Reflections on Landscape

If the world is a stage, then the landscape is the scenery – the stage set for the play. It is the setting for national and individual lives; and in so far as it is the result of human activities, it becomes a measure of underlying social structures.

Brenda Colvin, June 1942

Reflections on Landscape

The lives and work of six British landscape architects

edited by
Sheila Harvey

from interviews by Ian C. Laurie and Michael Lancaster

Gower Technical Press

Published by
Gower Technical Press Ltd,
Gower House,
Croft Road,
Aldershot,
Hants GU11 3HR,
England

Gower Publishing Company
Old Post Road
Brookfield
Vermont 05036
USA

British Library Cataloguing in Publication Data

Harvey, Sheila
    Reflections on landscape : the lives and
    work of six British landscape architects.
    1. Landscape architective - Great Britain
    - History - 20th century
I. Title
712'.092'2   SB470.55.G7

Library of Congress Cataloguing in Publication Data

Reflections on Landscape.
Work produced for the Landscape Institute.
Bibliography: P
1. Landscape Architects — Great Britain — Interviews.
2. Landscape Architecture — Great Britain.
3. Landscape.
I. Harvey, Sheila   II. Laurie, Ian C.   III. Lancaster, Michael.
IV. Landscape Institute.
SB469.9.R44   1987   712'.092'2   (B)   86-31923

ISBN 0 291 39708 5

Contents

Preface

The Landscape Institute (formerly the Institute of Landscape Architects) is a classic example of what can be achieved by a small group of determined enthusiasts, as this book shows. The initial impetus that led to the founding of the profession in 1929 took the form of a gathering of interested parties at the 1928 Chelsea Flower Show. One of those involved in this historic meeting was Brenda Colvin; when she died in 1981, the Institute's Library Committee was concerned that a wealth of personal experience and professional history would be lost. In fact, Sir Geoffrey Jellicoe now finds himself in the somewhat awesome position of being the last surviving founder member. The outcome was an attempt to create an oral history archive for the Landscape Institute by inviting senior members of the profession to subject themselves to a recorded interview, during the course of which they would discuss their lives and work and their views on various aspects of their chosen profession. Five interviews were completed between 1983 and 1985 and this publication is the result of a desire to bring the results to a wider audience. In order to reproduce for the reader the effect of listening to the speakers directly, the question and answer format of the original transcripts has been converted into continuous narrative. For the purpose of this book, the main editorial aim has been to retain the personality and spontaneity of the speaker as far as possible and to that end colloquial speech has taken precedence over written prose style. Each of the subjects had the opportunity to expand, condense or clarify what they had said in the original interview and was involved in the selection of illustrations.

The enormous changes that have taken place in this century are made apparent through both the lives and the work of the subjects. What is particularly striking in these informal autobiographical accounts is the development of firmly held views on design philosophy, education, social problems and, above all, the importance of co-operation between all persons concerned with the environment in whatever capacity; those who fought hard to establish the landscape profession feel strongly that the landscape itself is more important than professional rivalry. It is also a humbling experience to discover that many currently fashionable ideas about the environment were expressed by the subjects of this book long ago but, as is often the case with innovators, went unheard.

I should like to take this opportunity to acknowledge the contribution of some of the people involved in the preparation of this book. First of all credit is due to the Landscape Institute Library Committee, under the chairmanship of John Ford, for its initiative in setting up the interview project and, together with Jill Pearce of Gower Technical Press, for providing me with the chance of undertaking a stimulating and fascinating task. We are indebted to Ian Laurie for his hard work in the preliminary planning of the interviews and for personally interviewing Dame Sylvia Crowe, Brian Hackett, Peter Youngman and Sir Peter Shepheard; to Michael Lancaster for interviewing Sir Geoffrey Jellicoe; to Rosemary Fraser for help with transcribing and typing; and, of course, to the interviewees themselves who entered into the project, from which the Landscape Institute will benefit, with great enthusiasm and patience.

Finally, it seemed appropriate that a short chapter on Brenda Colvin should be included and I am extremely grateful to Hal Moggridge, her younger partner, from whose writings, notes and practice records this chapter is compiled. Grateful acknowledgement is also made to John Murray (Publishers) Ltd for permission to use an extract from Brenda Colvin's book *Land and Landscape.*

Sheila Harvey
June 1986

The illustrations originate as follows:

Facing page 1: Tara Heinemann; p.15; painting by Alan Sovull, exhibited at the Royal Academy in 1949; p.17: Susan Jellicoe; p.22: George Perkins; p.27: Lewis & Orgler; p.30: Jill Pearce; p.42 Cement and Concrete Association; p.46: Sylvia Crowe; pp.49, 50: John Brookes; p.52: Lord Snowdon; p.63: John Donat; pp.67, 77: Peter Shepheard; p.81: Ian Laurie; pp.85, 93: Brian Hackett; p.104: Watford Observer; pp.128-9, 131, 133, 135, 137: drawings by Michael Kemp; pp.140, 141, 146: Brenda Colvin; p.145: Chris Carter; pp.147, 148: Hal Moggridge; p.149: plan by Chris Carter, photo by David McQuitty; p.150: photo by David McQuitty.

Interviewer's Note

The interviews were carried out by Michael Lancaster and myself in the homes of the interviewees. They took the form of extended conversations based on a set of questions which I had prepared in consultation with the Library Committee of the Landscape Institute. The questions were sent in advance to the senior members concerned for approval and to enable them to prepare their thoughts. It was considered appropriate to use these questions as a loose framework and to follow a chronological sequence of topics with emphasis on the professional experience and achievements of the members. The questions were formulated on the basis of what I already knew of their careers from those writings and lectures which I had found rewarding during my own career in practice and teaching. In every case, our respect and admiration for the thoughts, ideas and experiences of the senior members interviewed provided a stimulus and motivation for the conversations, which we thoroughly enjoyed.

The conversations lasted about three hours each but were broken into two periods which were recorded on cassette tapes. These tapes were subsequently transcribed (by Pat Vaughan and June Atherton at the University of Manchester) and edited jointly by the interviewer and the senior member concerned before being submitted to the Landscape Institute with the unedited tapes. This method enabled a synoptic record to be made not only of the events in the members' lives but of their voices. It did not allow for discussion of the views held at any great length or depth, which could have been of additional interest.

Clearly, the interviewer must accept responsibility for the way he directed and controlled the conversations and for his ability to formulate and frame questions which would produce illuminating answers and stimulate the power of recall over many years in the minds of the members. Their capacity to do this was remarkable and tribute must be paid to the positive response that was given in all cases, along with the friendly spirit, good humour and warm hospitality offered to the interviewer, which did so much to create a suitably relaxed atmosphere for conducting the interviews.

Ian C. Laurie
June 1986

Sir Geoffrey Jellicoe

Sir Geoffrey is both architect and landscape architect and was Principal of the Architectural Association from 1939 to 1941. He was a founder member of the Landscape Institute and president from 1939 to 1949, as well as being a founder member and president of the International Federation of Landscape Architects in 1948. An interest in art is reflected in his being a member of the Royal Fine Arts Commission from 1954 to 1968 and a trustee of the Tate Galleries from 1966 to 73. Sir Geoffrey was awarded the CBE in 1961 and knighted for services to landscape architecture in 1979.

Early Life

I was born in 1900 in Chelsea and I have always liked to think of myself as a Cockney, if the wind be in the right direction from Bow Bells. My first memories were glimpses of my father at Rustington when I was two and then everything seems dark until I was five years old, when I remember quite clearly the building of a house at Rustington which included my first taking an interest in garden design. The general layout of the garden was done by my father, who was a publisher, but the interesting part of the garden was a wild garden with a wiggly-woggly path designed by my mother, who has always been my greatest influence. She was a student at the Slade School and I think somehow or other that this wild garden at Rustington was in some ways a preview of the ecological way in which people were thinking many years later. This was in 1905.

The art that I was most interested in as a child was writing, and my parents in fact thought that I was going to be a writer and I remember them giving me a marvellous fountain pen when I was 11 in order to encourage me. I went to a very good prep school when I was seven years old and stayed there for seven years. I remember, although I was by no means a good scholar, I had one phenomenal interest and that was Latin verse and so strong was this that when I was 12 or 13, I used to correspond during the holidays with another boy who shared my interest. We used to write to each other in Latin verse and, looking back, I think that the same sense of rhythm which this gave me has influenced one's classical feeling in art throughout one's life. We also did Greek at prep school.

At the age of 14 I got an exhibition to Cheltenham college. This was at the beginning of the war, and I went into the upper fifth, which was a very good start, but they cancelled Latin verse, the one thing that I was good at, and we did no further Greek. My learning while I was at Cheltenham was very slight; I wasn't taught to learn, I wasn't taught to be interested in learning, but I was interested in games. I did very well at games and in due course got into the cricket XI, became captain of gym and was very nearly in the first Rugby XV, but I was just beaten to it by another boy. I used to play on the right wing, a very fast runner, but I never got my 'first', although I did get my 'second'.

During this period, the war was going on of course, and one's future was entirely dominated by going into the Army and we were trained in the Officer Training Corps. However, I was 18 in October 1918 and on 11 November, the war came to an end. I left Cheltenham and had to decide, with my parents, what I was going to do. I really didn't know. I had obviously an interest in the arts, and in a fairly minor way I think, an interest in writing. I used to write stories, but you can't get a living out of writing stories, and in any case, none of them was ever published. What I did have published was a letter written to the *Daily Mail* from Cheltenham. It was a very good letter too, in my opinion. 'What makes a Gentleman?' was the current interest in the *Daily Mail* at that time. I said, and I still think it is extremely good, that gentlemen were 'those who gave up their seats in the underground railways, because the working class would never have the manners to do so, and the aristocracy would never travel underground', and this was published.

However, there was still the problem of a career and I had this very dramatic revelation at Christmas of 1918. I remember waking up in the morning and being absolutely certain that I wanted to be an architect. My parents agreed and within a few days I started at the Architectural Association, which was just beginning to get going after the war.

Strangely perhaps, the war didn't have a very strong effect on me. No one whom I was closely associated with was involved in the war apart from my brother and of course we were always very worried about him, but otherwise I think it was a curiously dead area from my point of view. One was devoted to games at Cheltenham and I still recall how very impressive were the cricket matches at this lovely college with its lovely landscape. The cricket pitch was a huge circle and the whole school used to sit round this tremendous circle of green whilst we batsmen had to go in and face the extraordinary situation of batting with six hundred people looking on. One always used to get pot funk but one enjoyed it and looking back on it, I can see that there was a grandeur about batting heroically in this huge circle with your whole school looking on. I was invited, I remember, to play at Lords, for the under 16s, but my parents couldn't raise the funds. I was in a holiday camp at the time, one of the agricultural camps which we went to.

Student Travels

When I went to the Architectural Association , there were a lot of people coming back out of the Army, people who had been fighting. They dribbled back, starting from the same time as I did, over the course of the next year, so the Architectural Association gradually built itself up into something more substantial. I think probably there were only about twenty there when I started in January 1918; certainly it was a very small number. The teaching was extraordinary. The 'modern movement' was going on in Europe at the time, but I don't think it seriously touched the Architectural Association. I remember even when I was in the third year, that we used to work with the plates from the Ecole des Beaux Arts, wonderful splendid designs on an heroic scale, and these we used to have beside us and we tried to copy them. I think it wasn't until the new principal Howard Robertson came to the AA with F. Yerbury as secretary, that the new world that was going on outside England began to dawn on us and the AA did lead the field in this revolution of conception. I remember old Professor Reilly of Liverpool University, which was a great rival to the AA, being absolutely devoted to the neo-classic, mainly Greek, and he couldn't understand what was happening at the AA, but the '20s was a period of great turmoil within the AA and by the end of the '20s the architectural revolution about the world had fully taken place. I was a student until 1923.

About 1922 or '23, four of us were in the final for a Rome scholarship. Of those four, only one really had any concept of what the modern world was about and that was Jock Shepherd, with whom I was later very closely associated. The three remaining people did designs which were accepted for the final competition but the only good design was by Jock Shepherd, a marvellous reinforced concrete design, which was thrown out by the RIBA! Howard Robertson had just been appointed at the AA and he took this up with them, and that was the moment of change, the throwing out of Jock Shepherd's design for a reinforced concrete bridge was when the modern movement revolution began.

Jock Shepherd was a far better designer than I could be – we all admired him a lot – and he won all the prizes at the AA school. When our courses ended he proposed that he and I should study and travel abroad for one year together. He was a man of means and I had none at all and he financed us (which ultimately I paid back) but it was his influence, I think, which can be said to be the most dominant in one's future career as a landscape architect. This came about because for our one year's travel abroad, we wanted to choose a subject, so we should not flitter from place to place, but have something serious to do. We asked our year-master, Leonard Bucknell, to tea at a café round the corner and asked him to advise us on what we could study. I had the idea of studying cathedrals, thinking of something vey grand, but he said 'well, there is a subject very few people know about and that is Italian gardens and the last serious book that was published was about 1820 by Percier & Fontaine; why don't you make a study of Italian gardens?' So we set off together with our drawing instruments and portfolios and rambled. We travelled hard the whole time, and travelling hard in those days was travelling hard; you had very uncomfortable railway journeys. But we set forth – we rambled through France and then we went into Italy. We had drawn up a list of gardens we wanted to visit which we got from various sources and I remember the first on our list was a place called Valzanzibio, near Venice. When we got there Jock Shepherd did all the photography, while I did all the measuring, which I did by pacing. As a side-line, I might say that I got so efficient at pacing after a year of studying Italian gardens in this way, that I was able to draw the sketch from which the pacing was made and produce a final version that was within 5 per cent of the actual correct dimensions. However, we visited Valzanzibio and that night in the local hotel I started to draw out the garden and we suddenly realised that we were into an extraordinary field of discovery, because as the drawing began to appear on paper, one realised the beauty of the actual plan and how it related to the site. In front of us was the discovery that Italian gardens could be transferred on to paper and from this, of course, came the standard work *Italian Gardens of the Renaissance* on which I did all the slogging work and Jock Shepherd did all the beautiful rendering. I think those drawings are still looked upon as very remarkable; they are now in the RIBA Heinz collection. This book, updated only by a long introduction by myself 60 years on, was republished by Academy Editions in 1986.

The gardens were in private hands and it was sometimes extremely adventurous getting into them. I remember at the Villa Piccolomini at Frascati we weren't allowed in, but we managed to get into the Villa to see the owners, who were having tea on the terrace, and Jock Shepherd – I suppose this was very naughty – kept them at bay by arguing (he was very good at argument) while I hastily made measurements. I suppose I was there about 15 minutes and got the major dimensions and the rest we were able to work out from bought photography. This has proved to be extremely useful, because the place was totally destroyed in the war and the only plans, as far as I know, were those I drew up.

We returned to England in 1924, touring slowly through Northern Europe and returning from Norway by a ghastly boat trip to Newcastle, where my brother met me. Jock and I separated there and I went on to Middlesbrough, where my brother was in business. I still remember the shock of arriving in Middlesbrough at that time – how sordid the whole city was. My brother looked after his works very well, but it was nevertheless a very terrifying experience after that marvellous year and I remember that night in Middlesbrough swearing that whatever I did, I would throw myself into landscape and try to make England a better place. There was naturally a certain amount of postwar euphoria in this resolution but the determination to devote oneself to landscape was very strong.

Setting up in Practice

Then we returned to London and Jock and I set up in practice and, in the usual way, had an awful struggle to survive. At first Jock Shepherd taught at the Architectural Association while I ran such practice as we had. We had got on extremely well together in writing the Italian gardens book – we were complementary to each other because I did the writing and the general organisation of it and he did the art side – but when we set up in practice, I began slowly to get a feeling of wanting to design for myself, I'd been totally dominated by him till then, although we did get on awfully well – we were eight years together in practice.

We started off by doing work on some domestic houses such as Paysdick, Patching, Sussex for Jock's mother, and Willey Broom Wood, near Caterham, Surrey, for old family friends of mine. These were awfully exacting things to do, and very difficult to make a living from, although some of it was quite interesting. But the most important contact at that stage arrived with a ring at the bell and there on the doorstep was a tall rather good-looking man with a new hat. This proved to be Gordon Russell and Gordon Russell remained a client for the rest of his life, until he died in 1980. He invited one of us, which in this case was me, down to Chipping Camden and I thought that this was an encouraging start but I sat in his garden all day and I went back on the train later without anything being settled at all. I wondered why he had invited me down as there didn't seem to be a job there. However, he was one of those people who was interested in people and, of course, in due time, I was invited down again to do a design for his works at Broadway and he became a lifelong friend and client. We had written a second book, published in 1927 called *Gardens and Design* which we didn't think much of at the time, because it was before the 'modern movement'. Looking back at it now, it was quite a good book and if you want to buy a second-hand copy, you'll have to pay a fabulous price for it today, but I don't think it is worth it. Anyway it was this book that introduced us to Gordon Russell, who said it was the best book on garden design he had ever read and therefore he wanted to meet its authors.

Then came the extraordinary case of Elizabeth Scott and the Shakespeare Memorial Competition, about 1930, or in 1931. Working in the office was a fellow student of Shepherd's called Alison Sleigh and Jock Shepherd, who was clearly attracted towards Alison, went along to the office to help Elizabeth Scott with her designs. He was such a very dominant character and such a good designer that he more or less tore up her scheme and did his own scheme. Elizabeth Scott, who realised that she was quite a good designer, but not all that good, accepted Jock's scheme. All this time, however, he and Alison were getting to know each other and in fact they became engaged and Elizabeth Scott won the Memorial Competition against the rest of the world. This was a terrific shake-up and Elizabeth acknowledged what Jock Shepherd had done by changing the title of the firm to Scott, Chesterton & Shepherd, Chesterton being the architect with whom Elizabeth Scott was working at the time. This was all very romantic and I remember quite well the excitement of winning that competition, but the result was that when they set up a proper office, there wasn't any place in it for me. I therefore decided that the time had come to cut adrift and set up on my own.

That would have been about 1932, and I had extraordinary luck because I got going almost immediately. Russell Page, who was working for Richard Sudell (a future president of the Institute of Landscape Architects, ILA), both of whom I had got to know because we were interested in landscape and were starting to found the Institute, came to the office one day and said 'I've got a client who really wants an architect to design his building for him and I'd like to have you.' It was a road-house in the Cheddar Gorge which sounded exciting to me and then it turned out his client was Viscount Weymouth, later Lord Bath, and I was even more excited. I went to town on that job and it was the only job of mine that's ever been shown in the Museum of Modern Art in New York. It is a completely modern design and was very well shown in the architectural journals and when I later came to stage two of the scheme (it was done in two stages), I invited all of the AA students I was then teaching, down for the opening; I had set them a parallel studio programme called 'Feddup Falls'. The scheme included the entrance and cafeteria building at Cheddar Gorge and there's a pool above the restaurant with a glass floor, which was considered very inventive. I think it has been a success and it is still there today.

Beginnings of the ILA

Going back to the foundation of the Institute of Landscape Architects in 1929, there was a gathering of Stanley Hart, Richard Sudell and Brenda Colvin and other interested persons at the Chelsea Flower Show of 1928. As a result of that, Sudell, who took the initiative at this stage, had arranged a meeting in his office in Gower Street. I remember it was on the top floor. He invited those people who were known to be interested in gardens which included me and Oliver Hill, I think, and Gilbert Jenkins, and we went to this meeting. Sudell was in the Chair, and it was then that we decided to found the Institute. Gilbert Jenkins whispered in my ear 'We must get Sudell out of the Chair and we must get Thomas Mawson in' and so at the next meeting, we proposed that although Sudell had done splendidly in starting the thing off, an Institute must have a great name to get it launched and Sudell was extraordinarily gracious and resigned from the Chair and Thomas Mawson, in name only, became the first president. Because of the prestige of his name, our small group grew. We then felt we must invite the two big names in landscape at this time , which were Prentice Mawson, son of Thomas Mawson, and Edward White to join, which they did. Joan Allen (Lady Allen of Hurtwood) also joined. The Institute was formally constituted in 1929, and I became the producer of *Landscape Notes*, some copies of which I believe exist at the library today, but that was a start. At the time of the Sudell meeting which was the first critical meeting, so far as I was concerned, I think there was no question that we took the American title which was 'landscape architects'. I always had doubts about this because we were then very much under the thumb of the architectural profession; all work for landscape architects came from architects and of course one endeavoured to break free. The great change came many years later with the title of The Landscape Institute, which made us completely independent of architecture; after all half of us are biological in any case and there are many planners too.

Pre-War Practice

Meanwhile the practice continued to expand. It was probably 1928 when I was still with Jock Shepherd that Avray Tipping, the architectural editor of *Country Life*, rang the bell and when I opened the door, he said 'I very much admire your Italian garden book and I'm advisor to a gentleman called Spier, Eugene Spier, a very wealthy man, who has bought Claremont. He's asked me to do everything: the interior, so that he can live like an English country gentleman and also the layout of the gardens. He wants swimming pools and proper entrance lodges and I would like you to advise on the landscape side.' Tipping wanted me rather than Jock Shepherd – I think I was much more genial than Jock – Jock was very difficult with clients, although once you got to know him, he was a very nice character. Anyway Avray Tipping wanted me and we went down to Claremont and had extraordinary times there. I remember on the second day, the whole of Claremont was empty and we went into the grand dining room and Tipping produced not only the butler, but a caseful of his family silver for a lunch party with Eugene Spier. The object of this was to show Eugene Spier how the English aristocracy lived and I remember this lunch party so very clearly in that otherwise empty place.

I got on with my designs and they were approved and a lot of money was going to be spent, for example there was to be an open-air swimming pool quite close to the house, which rather appealed to me at the time. The work was sent out to competitive tender and then poor Eugene Spier was squeezed on some vast international loan which he was financing and the points went down a peg, or half a per cent or something, and he was busted. The people who were in charge of his estate came along to see me about my fees and I must say that they paid up heroically, but that was the end of Eugene Spier and, as far as I was concerned, of Claremont. On the whole I think that it was probably for the best because the swimming pool, although I think it was quite well placed, would have slightly altered the character of the place, but I am not sure.

When I set up on my own in 1931, I went to a top floor in Bloomsbury Square which was handy for the AA, where I was teaching at the time. The AA teaching also provided some funds and I set up this place with furniture borrowed from my mother and two telephones, I remember. So that when someone rang up I would say, 'Oh yes, I'll see if Mr Jellicoe is in' and walk across the room to the other telephone and pick it up and say 'Yes, yes'.

About twelve months after the Cheddar Gorge job, the most serious of all clients suddenly appeared. This was someone called Ronald Tree who, through *Country Life*, had been recommended to me to lay out a new garden for an enormous Palladian building which he had just recently bought. He was immensely wealthy and had a lovely house in Queen Anne's Gate and I remember going down there and being quite frightened by the set-up: butler and footmen and so forth. Then I discovered that both he and Mrs Tree had each bought a copy of the Italian gardens book being passionately fond of Italian gardens, and the long and short of it was that I was asked down to Ditchley Park (which is now in the possession of the Anglo-American Institute) and was asked to lay out a garden in what was, for them, a grand manner.

Their house was a masterpiece of James Gibbs the architect, but there was certainly nothing of the garden at all when I went; there was a path, but no gardens around the house. They wanted a classical garden which I did for them, and because they were so eminent in the social whirl, I met everybody there. The parties that were held there were extraordinary. Ronald Tree remained one's patron, shall I say, right until the time of his death, when this was taken on by his son Michael, whom I used to know as a boy of twelve, and who is now in his 60s I suppose. He called me in for the house at Shute in the West Country which is a major work I have been doing over a period of ten years and is still going on at this moment, prior to one's culmination of landscape work at Sutton Place. The Tree family have been very loyal and when Ronald Tree wrote his autobiography he said that he had been doubtful whether Jellicoe could do this work, but that he was very satisfied and it was a very good job.

My landscape practice was growing at a great rate and through Ronald Tree, Russell Page and I got various introductions, including one to the Royal Lodge, Windsor, by the Duchess of York as she was then, and innumerable other Dukes and all sorts of people. Russell and I used to rush off together – he would do the planting and I would do the basic design. We weren't partners, we were just associated with each other and I learnt a lot from him and he, as he says in his autobiography, learnt a lot from me. I hope he did, but it was certainly a very exhilarating experience, working in these country houses – stately homes as they were really. Then, in the middle of this shemozzle going on in my practice, I met Susan Pares in 1936. I fell for her immediately and we were married in July 1936 and she became associated with the work I was doing, although she didn't really become closely associated with it until after the war.

We met when I advertised for a secretary, getting very grand ideas, and she was drawn to the advertisement by her interest in the arts, and architecture and landscape generally. She was in the office until the war – I was very lucky to get her – she was very high-powered indeed, but I think she was drawn, as I say, towards the subject. I used to call Russell Page and Susan, 'Dilly' and 'Tante', because they were very amusing together. She was an intellectual and he was very artistic-minded and they got on together extraordinarily well. Eventually he made a speech at our wedding – he wasn't the best man but we asked him to make a speech – and he got up, said 'I am not going to make a speech' and sat down again, much to everybody's amusement. This was very typical of Russell.

The practice still had a lot of architecture going on because landscape wasn't paying; it wasn't yet a viable proposition. Again via Ronald Tree, one got one of the biggest jobs one ever had and that was the Bestwood Colliery round about 1938. We never made any money in the office before the war, it just ticked over; it was quite impossible in those days to make money because it was just domestic landscape. You lost money right, left and centre but took on the jobs because it was awfully good experience and I maintain that anyone who can design a small garden can design a big town quite easily.

Teaching at the AA and the Second World War

In the early '20s there was just Jock Shepherd teaching at the AA until I went back to teach the third year. Teaching on the drawing board, which I loved, changed my whole attitude. In those days, when you taught, you went to a person's drawing board and practically did it yourself. There was a maestro at work and the student, unless he was a very good student, needed guidance to design. This was very stimulating to the mind and I think one's interest in modern work and Corbusier stems from these students who introduced me to the idea of Corbusier. A group of them calling itself Tecton eventually became famous in their way and in fact built Highpoint in which I now live. It was what I got from the students which really fired me away from neoclassicism. Jock Shepherd always said he was not a modernist himself, although I think he pointed the finger towards modernism, he was half-way between the two. At the AA by that time, through the influence of Corbusier and the Bauhaus and so forth, you were in a modern world.

By 1939, the AA was in a most awful pickle. The students had revolted and wouldn't put up with the existing teaching. They searched to find replacements and the only two personalities, not necessarily wanting to be teachers, who came within range, were Maxwell Fry and myself. I had a very strong feeling that I ought to apply and was further encouraged to do so by the considerable struggle to make ends meet in the office. I was also very fond of the AA – when you have been a student of the AA you get awfully fond of it for life. I was accepted and became principal of the AA at £1000 a year for four days a week. I laid on a private telephone between my office and my room at the AA which never worked, but it was nice to know one had a private line, it made one feel important. Then the war came and I took a car and announced that I wouldn't be back until I had found a place for the AA to be evacuated to. I went to various places in north London and eventually saw a nice house in Barnet. I knocked on the door and I said 'Can we have your house for the duration of the war for this school of architecture?' and they said 'Certainly you can.' I went back wholly surprised to the Council and that night, more or less, the contract was signed and the school moved out there for the duration of the war and very nice it was too.

I always remained at Grove Terrace and I remember the journeys back sometimes with the raids going on in London and shrapnel falling from the heavens from our own guns, much more dangerous than the bombs. I used to go out to Barnet every day, but I never liked it; I don't think I am competent to be an organiser on that scale and I used to be totally exhausted. The result was that after three years as principal of the AA, I threw in my hand – I quarrelled a great deal with the Council too over all sorts of things; it was a very emotional place – and I proposed that Frederick Gibberd, whom I had appointed to the staff, should take my place. He only lasted a couple of years too and I said that no principal of the AA could last more than a couple of years.

With the coming of the war, the Russell Page world totally collapsed so we broke up the partnership and I was on my own again from the beginning of the war, although I had taken a student from the AA called Richard Wilson and someone called Ellen Heckford who acted as secretary, both for me and, for a time, to the Institute of Landscape Architects. Then the war work opened up for me on a very big scale and the practice expanded tremendously. There was an enormous amount of work, housing for the Ministry of Works, and I had eight sites throughout the south of England. My staff was up to about 40, the largest I ever had or wanted, and at the same time we were also appointed to deal with bomb repairs in the Islington area of London. We were still living in Grove Terrace where we had been since we were married, and I remember that whenever a bomb fell – you could hear a bomb falling in that direction – I thought 'this means another thousand or two in one's pocket.' This was so horrible that I decided then that any profit I made during the war would be put to some good use like landscape and that was why one financed landscape during the war.

ILA and IFLA

In 1939, I followed Thomas Adams as president of the ILA; because there wasn't much landscape work going on, I could run it from my office. This is described in my chapter in the publication *50 Years of Landscape Design* which deals with the Institute journal which we kept going during the war years. One did no landscape work during the war, obviously, but one did help to keep the Institute alive. In fact I remained president until 1949 and in 1948 became the founding president of the International Federation of Landscape Architects.

That, of course, was another dramatic moment. The Landscape Institute had called an international meeting to be held at County Hall in 1948, which was the result of an earlier meeting of the Landscape Institute, at which Joan Allen had popped up and said 'let's call an international meeting and possibly have an international federation arising from it.' We all agreed – it sounded awfully easy – and the motion was passed. It was really quite something, that first meeting in 1948. We had County Hall and many eminent people were there – I remember the Minister at the time was Lord Silkin who was invited to attend and declined but when he realised that such a distinguished body was going to be present he rang up at the last moment and said he would like to come after all. Then all of the delegates moved to Cambridge and it was at Jesus College, Cambridge that we founded the IFLA, with me as president, Sylvia Crowe as the honorary secretary and Brenda Colvin as the representative of England, and that's where it all started.

Post-War Practice

Another one of those extraordinary happenings resulted in my practising in Rhodesia, between 1948 and 1952. During the war when I was involved in this housing work, I employed some of the major contractors in this country and I got on with them awfully well – we did an entire housing scheme with one firm in eight weeks. Anyway some time after the war, I was sitting in the office at Gower Street when the telephone rang and a voice said 'You won't remember me but I was your contractor for such and such a scheme and I am sending a number of people to Rhodesia, central Africa, because I think there is a great development possibly there; will you come?' I said 'Well I don't know, Rhodesia is a long way off and I've never done anything like this before.' It was about noon and he needed to have a decision by 1 o'clock. It meant going out and setting up in practice in Rhodesia, which in those days was much farther off than it is today, because you couldn't go by air and of course I had to consult my wife. I tried to reach Susan on the telephone to get her advice, which was always sought on occasions like this, but she wasn't in and I had no alternative but to make a decision myself. The only person left in the office was the girl operating the telephone and I remember quite clearly walking out and saying 'I've got the offer of this vast job in Rhodesia, do you advise me to take it?' She was called Miss Tarrier and she looked at me and said 'Of course you should.' I jumped into a taxi and met the contractors for lunch and said 'I'll take on this job.'

Susan was rather breathless when she heard but of course she agreed that it was inevitable if one was of an adventurous frame of mind – and of course I have always been all for adventure whenever possible – that I should go. Apart from the tour of Italy, there had been holidays abroad, but nothing like this, where one was throwing oneself into this totally new world and getting there. Fortunately I knew Lord Reith very well; he'd been a great supporter of the Landscape Institute in its formation, and he organised my travel by military plane as far as Egypt, I think it was; anyway I got there much faster than the contractors. We arrived in Northern Rhodesia at Lusaka and we stayed – I took Susan with me – in an appalling hotel but fortunately, again, one had links with the Governor and he came to our rescue by inviting us to stay at the Governor's house for the rest of the time we were there.

I decided while I was there that I would set up in practice and then came the extraordinary adventures of bringing staff with families out there. Of course I hadn't got the money to finance them, but the government gave us an advance for this work because we were working on a government contract. It was a mixture of hospitals, schools and the international airport at Livingstone but mainly schools, I would say, because we had four or five schools in the Copper Belt to do. All of these had to have separate offices and were inaccessible by telephone so I tried to set up a private wireless between them which you could do in those days. There was little or no landscape work involved, since the whole of one's contract was architectural, but obviously, in the placing of buildings, one took great care. One major work was an hotel in Lusaka (getting a decent hotel for once) and we did make it the best hotel in Africa for the time being. That related to its landscape with pools and things like that, but by and large the work was architectural, except for the new town plan for Lusaka that I did, which called upon certain landscape qualities. My contract was to go out there for a fortnight, twice a year; in the meantime the main work was still going on in England.

I remember one's most interesting and curious job at the time was the gardens round the house at Sandringham and this was a very high-powered thing because I would go and spend a weekend there in a world which was far removed from one's daily life. It was a lovely feeling having the train stopped specially for one at the local station, which you were entitled to do. Of course one's relations with the Royal family, with the late King, were very close and they went on until he died.

By this time one had built up quite a practice. Hemel Hempstead New Town came in at that stage, about 1947, and this was quite a dramatic moment: Frederick Gibberd and I were appointed on the same day. He having Harlow and I choosing Hemel Hempstead, because I had the first choice and I chose Hemel Hempstead because Lord Reith was chairman and Reith had been a tremendous help to the Landscape Institute behind the scenes. He had been on the Council at one stage when I was president, a frightening experience to have someone of that stature as a member, but he was very good indeed, so much so that we tried to persuade him to follow me as president, but he wouldn't and we had Thomas Sharp instead who was very good indeed. We had a whole lot of people who were working behind the scenes to build up the Institute's prestige when Silkin was Minister of Town and Country Planning, as I think it was called then, and when new towns appointments were made we were in a position to see that every new town had its landscape architect. That period around the end of the '40s and the beginning of the '50s was a great period for the opening up of the profession as a whole. For instance, Lord Holford, who was a member of the Council, had tremendous influence with the Central Electricity Generating Board in getting it to appoint landscape architects.

Writings and Influences

My ambitions for the profession were being fulfilled; one could see clearly the way it was going to develop and in fact had developed, but on a personal level, I don't think one began to feel really fulfilled until recently, till I retired or reached the age of 80.

I'd had a period in the '20s and early '30s when I had written about four books, including *Italian Gardens, Garden Ornament* and some books which weren't frightfully good, and then I had a very long pause until after the war. I was beginning to accumulate theories and I started on *Studies in Landscape Design* which I produced at a rate of one every three or four years. Later on, with Susan, came *The Landscape of Man* which took us 17 years to write and was started about 1957 and was published in 1975. I knew it was going to take a very long time because I had to do all the research and one's holidays, once a year, were spent in travelling to about every place illustrated in the book. I produced statistics showing what I'd do by such and such a date and it took about five years longer than I had anticipated, although I had planned for about twelve years.

There were four men who influenced me profoundly. The first was Jock Shepherd, the second was Gordon Russell, the third was Frederick Gibberd and the fourth, possibly the most influential in later life, was Ben Nicholson. There are all sorts of other people, too many for me to recount, who influenced me also, to a lesser degree. For example, I appreciated what Christopher Tunnard was doing in attempting to initiate a modern landscape to parallel the modern movement in architecture, and I tried to get him to teach at the AA just before the war, because I knew he had a message to give to the younger generation which I couldn't at that time understand. He stirred one up with his first book – which is now a classic – because there is a small reproduction in it of one of my drawings from *Gardens and Design* which is obviously included somewhat cynically as an example of what is old hat. I've always rather enjoyed that because I like being given a step forward particularly where landscape is concerned. I knew Tunnard personally and liked him very much.

Up to the time after the war I had been passionately interested in historic works, paintings and so forth. It wasn't until I met Frederick Gibberd about 1948/49 and saw his collection of modern paintings and couldn't understand them in the slightest, that suddenly through talking with him, discussing things with him, a completely new window was opened for me. In his home, which was next door to us in Grove Terrace, he had prints by Paul Klee and Nicholson and he was beginning a collection, which is now a very good one, of modern works. I then started buying modern paintings for myself on two accounts: one is that I fell passionately in love with a picture and second is that it was by an already famous name. One can easily kid oneself into seeing things in a modern painting which exist in one's mind, but which don't really exist in the actual drawing. If you buy with the knowledge that other people have recognised this as great art and you like it, then you are on absolutely safe ground. That is why I used to allocate a small sum of money each year, about £100 or so, to one picture and this is how one built up one's own collection which is quite valuable. Frederick used to say that putting modern art on the walls supplied him with a sort of electric impulse which never stopped. Some of my pictures I have had some 30 years now I suppose and they are still absolutely vivid, the artist's feeling projects itself into one.

For some years I was on the Fine Arts Commission which I enjoyed very much but it wasn't until I became a trustee of the Tate Gallery that I was again forced to study my own feelings and responses to modern work. I loved it and the monthly meetings we had there were very dramatic because you had to sum up quickly your feelings about whether such and such a thing was worth purchasing. I used to get stumped every now and then, in fact a lot, with items I just didn't understand, but I used to say so and not vote, or I would give my vote to the director, because the director wouldn't have put it up for consideration unless he thought it was very good anyway. If I distinctly disliked a painting I would reject it but at other times one felt that something was a great work of art. Every time one felt that emotion, so one's experience was developing, and that period at the Tate Gallery was, from my point of view, the most enriching of all experiences I think I have ever had.

Hemel Hempstead

But to return to 1948, when I was appointed landscape consultant to Hemel Hempstead, this again was one of the dramatic moments in one's life. I received a letter from the Minister saying 'Will you design the new town of Hemel Hempstead? You will complete in one year and your fee will be one thousand pounds.' Of course, one absolutely jumped at this. Frederick Gibberd had had a similar letter for Harlow and we met the Minister at the same time. The designs for Harlow and Hemel Hempstead were running parallel to each other and they had to be completed at the same date, which we did, and there then occurred another of the dramatic moments in my life when I realised that Frederick Gibberd's designs for Harlow were a world apart from mine. Mine was alright – it wasn't classicism but it had a great sense of classicism in it – but it belonged to the past. Frederick Gibberd's design, however, looked like a work of art, the plan itself, the drawings and so forth were influenced strongly by Ben Nicholson, whom he knew and admired and whose work he had examples of. The predominant thing about the plan was the sense of landscape and his scheme went ahead and, in fact, was more or less built as he had planned. It didn't come out as well as one had hoped, certainly, but I don't think that was his fault. Mine of course was modified and altered and changed about and didn't stand the test of time and the reason was because I think it was backward-looking.

I always kept on very good terms with Hemel Corporation, in spite of quarrelling with them quite a lot, and about seven years later they asked me to design a water scheme. The chairman asked me to have a drink with him at the Hyde Park Hotel and I remember distinctly we went into the bar and he said 'I'd like you to come and do the water garden scheme at Hemel Hempstead' and I said 'Not on your life, after the experiences I have had with your Corporation.' After another gin and tonic I eventually agreed that I would take on the job on one condition, namely, that the chairman would support whatever I did through thick and thin and in fact he did. That's how it came about, but it was a toss-up over whether one was going to do it, because one had been so mauled about on the housing work I did there; one's original scheme had been messed about – quite rightly in some ways – but anyway the water garden became one of the jobs that I look back on as being successful.

Susan worked with me on Hemel Hempstead. She had been

Unexecuted design for the centre of Hemel Hempstead New Town 1948.

a housewife before the war and had a remarkable war career in the Ministry of Information but after the war was over she thought she ought to participate in some way in the work that I was doing. Because of her interest in planting she started to do all my planting work and Hemel Hempstead was the first major work that she did − she did all the planting there. We've still got the planting plans for it which I think were very successful and from that time until the completion of Sutton Place quite recently, my wife has done all my planting. Susan's wartime experiences stimulated her tremendously and she wrote books both on her own and in collaboration with Lady Allen, and me of course.

In 1951 I did quite a considerable housing scheme, the Lansbury Neighbourhood Housing Scheme in Poplar, which was an architectural venture, nothing to do with landscape, but I think I missed out on the Battersea Gardens for the Festival of Britain which went to Russell Page, because I had fallen out with the organiser, Gerald Barry, about a year or two before the Festival of Britain schemes were being prepared. The *News Chronicle* had organised a remarkable design modelled for the town of Knutsford, and they got four architects working on this scheme, all eminent like Frederick Gibberd and Francis York and I was appointed landscape architect over the whole area. Gerald Barry, who was the editor of the *News Chronicle*, inspired this scheme (and, in fact, inspired the Festival of Britain proposals) and while he liked my total scheme very much, he disagreed on one point. There was an area round the lakes near the factories which I had kept pure green grass and the factory workers weren't allowed to go on to this because I didn't want it spoilt. Now he said they ought to be able to use this area for lunchtime recreation and this was a significant moment in social history, because in a way he was quite right. Here was this green grass, here were the factory workers − why shouldn't they have their sandwiches sitting by the lake? But I said that they would spoil it all and I wouldn't budge so because of that I lost the Battersea job. However, I met Gerald Barry some time after and we were very good friends, but in this life you must every now and then stand on a principle and this was a principle I wasn't going to give way on.

About this time I was also involved in a plan for a cement works. The chairman of the Hope Valley Cement Works, Sir George Earle, was interested in landscape and in trying to ensure that industrial buildings were seemly in the landscape. He called upon me, during the war, in the temporary office I had − we'd been bombed out − and asked me to tackle this. The long and short of it was that we had a frightfully good model made in the office by the office boy, showing limestone cliffs that really looked like cliffs and Sir George fell for this model and, as a result, supported everything I did then and ever since. He was a pioneer of the concept of planning ahead in industry in so far as it affected the landscape. I was called in about 1980 to do a reassessment of the plan and I felt that while they hadn't followed my plan entirely they had followed the principles one had laid down, then swerved for unforeseeable practical reasons in a different direction, which I thought was awfully good. It was extremely interesting 30 or 40 years later, to see how very well this had worked.

Towards a
Philosophy of Landscape

About the middle of the '50s, I began to get interested in the subconscious in landscape design and some of one's previous work, like the Hemel Hempstead water gardens, was based on this idea. When the Kennedy Memorial came along in 1964, it gave me my first serious opportunity of seeing whether it was possible to put a subconscious idea into a work, so that it is more important and more lasting than the purely visual impression the eye receives. We had very little money for the Memorial because, quite correctly, the bulk of the money was set aside for a scholarship fund and therefore, it was only symbolic of an idea, although I would like to think it has been the basis of one's work ever since.

When you go to the Kennedy Memorial, you will see it's quite nice visibly, and if it is a fine day, it's very pleasant there, but subconsciously you are actually being told the story of the Pilgrim's Progress. Its theme controlled every piece of detail, like for instance the 60 000 granite setts going up to the memorial which were all hand cut, all quite different one from another, and represent individuals making their way to the Memorial. The stonemason who was laying it laid his setts beautifully, but I asked him not

Kennedy Memorial, Runnymede 1965.

to lay them in a military, regimented fashion, but to lay them like crowds at a football match, where each one is an individual. I won't go into the full story of the Kennedy Memorial, except to say that the concept behind the symbolism was of a pilgrimage which ran through the whole design until you got to Jacob's ladder with its steps to heaven. This was fairly successful with people who didn't know anything about the allegory, in that they might become aware that they were experiencing something much greater than what they actually saw. It also set me off on work which one is now beginning to do on a very big scale indeed and is being accepted by the public as such.

Soon afterwards, in 1966, I had a curious battle over the Crematorium at Grantham. I got the landscape right, I think, with the cross and so forth, but not the actual building because I was still looking back at what crematoria were – rather sad things. I remember quite well my partner, Francis Coleridge, writing to me while I was away on holiday and saying that he didn't really think that this was the right philosophy; it wanted to be something cheerful. He did a design which I liked very much and I went to a meeting with the Grantham Committee and told them that I'd given the matter a great deal of thought and that although my design was alright, I thought its philosophy was completely wrong. I then told them that I'd had a complete revolution of mind and tore up my drawings before the Committee. They were rather amazed, but accepted the final proposal which I liked very much, of Francis Coleridge's building and my landscape.

Francis came as assistant about 1948, and we developed a very big practice. There was a lot of work going on – various civic centres and things like that – and I also had another partner Alan Ballantyne who stayed until about the beginning of the '70s. He had been in charge of the Plymouth Civic Centre and had an office there and he obviously wanted to continue working as an individual.

Other Projects

I think I had built up a certain reputation through my plan for the Parish of Broadway in 1933, which was the first of its kind under the new Town & Country Planning Act. In 1945, just at the end of the war, I was asked to do a plan for Wolverton in Buckinghamshire which was the first town plan I had ever tackled – Wolverton is now of course absorbed into the new town of Milton Keynes – but this again I think added to one's reputation. There were very few specialist town planners in the country at the time and this led to my being appointed to do Hemel Hempstead New Town in 1948. In fact there were a whole number of town plans which included Guildford and parts of Edinburgh.

One I remember best is that for Gloucester, which was prepared with Hal Moggridge as assistant. Hal had worked with me for a long time and he made the most beautiful models of Gloucester new town on which he worked very hard indeed. It is the only town plan which still carries out certain of one's views in what is known as the Via Sacra, which is a way round the centre of Gloucester, passing all the famous historic buildings and linking the whole idea of Gloucester into one scheme. This had been so successful that 21 years later I was invited to a very pleasurable ceremony, an evening there – Hal came down with me – when the 21st birthday of the Jellicoe plan was celebrated.

Hal also worked with me on some of the Pilkington projects, known as the 'glass age' projects and these purely imaginative schemes were financed by Pilkington Brothers to create designs for something that would not be done for 50 years, but *could* be done at the present day knowing what materials and so forth were available and Hal's imagination played a considerable part in these various schemes. These included a glass bridge across the Thames at Vauxhall and a glass exhibition tower at King's Cross. One of them, which showed all roads on the roofs and only landscape on the ground, Motopia, had a book published about it entirely. When I visited Japan, I found that the influence of the 'glass age' committee designs, which were negligible in this country, were very considerable in Japan; in fact they had partly built a Motopia there. Sea City, a new town in the North Sea off Yarmouth, was the final project and although the conception was mine, it was Hal who worked it out. This was the last of the great Pilkington schemes – all the models I believe are up at St Helens, Pilkington's headquarters – and they do show a remarkable range of imaginative thought.

In 1965 I received a commission for a landscape plan for the Isles of Scilly. Anybody's heart would have jumped at the idea of islands and doing plans for islands. I took about a year doing this plan and I used to think that I had never met any landscape which is quite so romantic as this cluster of islands in the sea, with the rise and fall of the tides, so that the landscape is always changing. My job really was one of conservation. I had to understand what it was that attracted visitors there and then I laid down certain rules, which I called a 'Charter for the Isles of Scilly' and these still hold. A new economic plan is being made at this moment (1985), all particulars of which have been sent to me, and I was delighted to see that they were simply carrying on where I left off. One had to relate a very tremendous piece of natural landscape to the doings of man and man of course does change with the times. It wasn't preservation; it was more conservation. How to sustain the ethos of the islands without it being destroyed by speculators and the major thing, which has been very difficult indeed, was to restrict the population coming in, so that you have only a limited number of people using the islands at all.

This was followed by a plan for Sark in the Channel Islands, I think the most romantic work one has ever done. First of all it was very difficult to get there and secondly, it is quite a small island with massive cliffs all the way round which have been its natural defence, and finally it is one of the few areas in what we might call the British world, which is self-governing. They are only responsible I think to the Monarch, as is the Dame of Sark who rules the island (she has since died), and the families of the 40 people who own the island date back to Elizabethan days when it was taken over and divided up. I can't tell you how much I like the people of Sark, they were absolutely delightful, but one's scheme fell flat on the ground, when it ultimately dawned upon them that they would have to give away some of their land in the public interest, which is normal planning procedure anywhere else in the world. The people of Sark have this strong feeling of love of ownership of their land and courteously allowed me to pass from one estate to another, from one farmland to another, even though they didn't allow each other to pass without asking the owner's permission. The Rights of Ownership are still the most powerful thing in Sark and this makes it one of the most interesting islands — a world of its own. I love Sark very much, but all I have influenced is the use of materials and that sort of thing as part of the basic strategy for coping with visitors; their wealth had changed from agriculture to visitors and this of course is the most dangerous thing for the destruction of the ethos of a place. What is happening now I am not quite sure, but if they are wise they will keep their own extraordinary sense of *place* in Sark, which is what attracts visitors and they will have to handle those visitors as best they can, without letting them trample on them or the land values. They can't sell the land without general permission; they do protect themselves in that way, otherwise the place would be filled with foreigners by this time.

This problem of visitors and conservation is a problem which occurred very early on with my plan in 1933 for Broadway in Worcestershire. You have to take into account that Broadway had changed totally from when the present aesthetic of buildings among the hills had been formed, that is to say its wealth now lay in visitors and you had to handle these visitors in such a way that they didn't destroy the very thing they came to see. I drew up the plan in 1933 and I've been in contact with it ever since. With very little variation, they have continued on the principles laid down at the time and I am very pleased that this should be so because it's a marvellous landscape and it would be a great pity to destroy it.

In principle it is very close to what I had originally designed. The intention was that the great curve of the hills in which it lies should be retained as pure landscape, a very shapely landscape created in the 18th century but not obviously a park, whilst the stone buildings of the village itself remain as beautiful as ever. There are some extra car parks and things away from the hills, but it's very unobtrusive. The numbers of cars in the High Street, or what one calls the High Street, but it's the main road, were at first acceptable; then of course they grew and grew and so car parks were made in an area where they didn't obtrude. It means that you have to walk quite a step from the car park to the village, but people ought to be prepared to do that. By and large Broadway has looked after itself pretty well. This I think is largely due to the Russell family, because Gordon set up his works there and his father owned the Lygon Arms Hotel which is now one of the best in England, and it is in the interests of the traders and everybody there that Broadway should be preserved, because this is what attracts visitors.

Earth Sculpture

Going back to more recent work, one of the items which everybody notices when travelling on the Great West Road is the Guinness Hills at Park Royal. This was the first modern attempt to use waste soil in a constructive way. In 1959, I was asked by the Guinness Company to prepare landscape plans for the site left over after the motorway which runs through it had been made. This was a very awkward site, criss-crossed with two railways and roads and I didn't know what to do – you had to do something which was very outstanding – and then I saw the soil being dug from the underpass on the outer circular road which passes straight by and I thought to myself, instead of spending a fortune in carrying that subsoil away to dump it about three or four miles off, why can't I use it to make a hill? I asked Guinness whether they agreed and they were very thrilled by the idea and we made the first of two hills, which I don't think is particularly interesting. It was just a conical hill filling a rather difficult site, very dominating, but from the making of that hill, I realised that there could be, when remodelling land, a sculptural form; it should have a sense of sculpture. It is, I think, pretty good and the two combined are quite entertaining as you flash by on that road; it gives the appearance that the road was diverted by the hills, rather than the hills coming after the road. Rather like Silbury, it gives added dignity to the hills.

Harwell came soon after that and by now one was getting very interested in sculptural form. From 1954 to 1968 I was on the Royal Fine Arts Commission and I used to sit next to Henry Moore whom I had known for many years, and I told him I'd got this commission for disposing of 350 000 tons of chalk at Harwell from the excavations. He thought that this was a marvellous chance for sculpture in the landscape, so one set about designing those chaotic waste dumps into separate hills. It was extremely interesting because one had to plan these hills so that you did a tour right the way round them; they fell into different compositions. I think Harwell was one's earliest experiment in pure sculpture of the landscape, at discovering what landscape architects can do. Another development on the same lines occurred with the Cheltenham Sports Centre in 1968. Once one got the idea, of course, and I had given a talk about the Guinness Hills to the Royal Institute of British Architects, I think it set a lot of people thinking that waste soil need not be waste soil; it can be very constructive indeed. This is what happened at Cheltenham, it was a development of the idea and one has since then done innumerable hills and indeed other people have done finer hills, like the Liverpool International Garden Festival in 1984, where you see a whole range of hills.

I was also working at Oldbury-on-Severn nuclear power station in 1960. Here I was influenced by the artist Ben Nicholson, whom I didn't know at the time, although I knew his work and had always been thrilled by its pure geometry. The Harwell hills were biological, but the Oldbury Hill was flat; it wasn't a hill at all, it was the disposal of three quarters of a million tons of soil from digging up the River Severn to form a reservoir of cooling water.

I had the greatest fun in designing what I call an abstract pattern of fields and it got a long way towards completion before the engineers suddenly discovered that they had mis-calculated the amount of soil that was coming from the river, some of which had been swept away by the tidal movement of the sea. The result was that they hadn't got enough soil to complete my scheme, so if anyone goes to Oldbury, they will see it three-quarters done; the rest is a kind of ruin.

Ben Nicholson's Wall

I got to know Ben Nicholson in 1963, because I wrote an article about his work in *Studio International* and he was so thrilled by this that we made contact and remained fast friends until his death in 1984. I also spent a lot of money in buying one of his works from the Marlborough Galleries, which I have with me now, just a few lines and a daub of colour. It seemed then a huge sum to pay, but I was really profoundly moved by it and he was moved by the fact that I had spent this money on one of his works and had written this article which was very understanding of what he was trying to do.

The Nicholson Wall, Sutton Place, Guildford 1982.

One of the things Ben Nicholson always wanted to do was to build what he called 'a wall': in many of his publications the abstract design is called 'design for wall' and I was determined that this should be done. I got a grant from the Arts Council for £2000 towards the making of the wall and his fee and then we set about trying to find a suitable place. I tried many places, the Cement and Concrete Association, Sussex University and a site on the South Bank, which either Ben wouldn't agree with the siting or the money wasn't available to complete the job. Then we settled on Cheltenham, where I was building some swimming pools and the landscape round about and it seemed an ideal situation. Ben came down and agreed that this was the site that he would like. Then we set about carrying it out. This we knew would be very difficult technically, and Ove Arup, our advisor, gave great thought to the problem for he too was a great admirer of Ben Nicholson's work. However, it could not be done without the risk of it not surviving more than a summer because the materials could only be of the cheapest of concrete. We got the surface working alright, thanks to the experiments of Mrs June Harrison who was working in my office at the time and she says, in fact, that she still has in her garden in Hampstead the original sample, which has been out in the open air and has survived up to now. The fear was that this delicate surface would be destroyed by the winter conditions and if so I, as advising architect, would certainly be sued by the local authority for giving wrong advice and spending their money. The Cement and Concrete Association put a tremendous amount of thought into the research, trying exactly to get one of his paintings turned into reality. They went to the Tate Gallery to study, they made samples and so forth at their research works, but Ove Arup was quite right in saying that what we had got was only a surface treatment and would not stand the test of time, when we wanted something that would be there for a couple of hundred years, and this could not be guaranteed. This was achieved later in marble at Sutton Place where money was no object and will last for two hundred years at least.

Still at Cheltenham I became involved with the College of Art and Design when I was appointed governor. I was very keen when I was building the swimming pool that the School of Landscape Design and of Painting should form part of the scheme. I commissioned the school to do a series of panels but I think the good people of Cheltenham just didn't understand them. They were remarkably inexpensive – they were financed by a society which was associated with the Royal Academy, but I don't think the local authority had any idea what it was meant to be; it was, in fact, rather futuristic.

Retirement

During the '60s and '70s one was doing interesting work, but only what I call 'ticking over' in design. In 1973, the partnership ceased, I closed the office and one retired to one's home, where one thought one would probably lead a quiet old age. '*The*

Landscape of Man' (re-published 1986 and updated since 1975) was the last major work one ever hoped to do and that was published in 1975. I set up my office at home, not expecting to do very much work, but of course a creative artist just goes on for ever; he never stops. I had a kind of sabbatical seven years, there was a certain amount of work going on, but it was mainly modest gardens.

I hadn't done any teaching or been closely associated with students since I'd been at the Architectural Association (not as principal, but in the third year) when Michael Lancaster invited me to a day's seminar at Thames Polytechnic at Hammersmith. I went in such fear and trepidation as to whether I could get on with students. However, I found that associating with the students could be extremely stimulating, provided they are good students and they cross-question you, which is excellent experience for the elderly. When Thames Polytechnic moved to Dartford I followed, so to speak, and until quite recently, I used to go there to conduct a day's seminar and very much enjoyed it. It was very hard work indeed, you had to keep your wits about you to understand what the students were doing and why, what their standards are, and I found their discussions of any criticism particularly stimulating. I suppose by that time I was approaching 80.

It wasn't until I was 80 years old that the world, as far as I was concerned, was turned completely upside down. Two very large jobs came in, almost simultaneously, in the summer of 1980. One was Sutton Place, where Hugh Casson, who was president of the Royal Academy at the time, was doing the interior, and had recommended me to do the outside. I remember I wasn't sure if I really wanted to do it, because I was picking and choosing the work I was going to do and I had no staff. I decided to go down at any rate and see what a Texas millionaire is really like, although I thought it might not be my cup of tea, but within ten minutes of meeting it became obvious that we were batting on the same wicket. He was interested in all that I had been exploring into the subconscious in recent years: can you put the subconscious into landscape design in the same way that an artist can express the true meaning of what he is trying to do through the pictorial representation? I was being offered the opportunity to design landscape on a scale which I had never thought of before. If you take all the gardens one has done in the past and multiply them by ten you will get some idea of what the expenditure at Sutton Place has been. As far as Stanley Seeger was concerned expense was no object, but quality was and not only quality of mind, but quality of technique and materials.

Well, the long and short of it was the success of Sutton Place put me in the international field in no uncertain way. Visitors going there experience what I was trying to do, that is to say I wanted to give them an experience which is greater than life. There are beautiful vistas, the landscape of course is very nicely done and jolly well ought to be after 60 years of experience, but it is not that, it's what lies behind it all, so that about three or four days after a visitor goes there, it should hit him that he has had a transcendental experience! One has made contact with the public in a way one could never normally do in planning and landscape and so forth.

Sutton Place was designed originally for an individual, Stanley Seeger, and is now run by a trust, but the brief has remained identical, that is to say, it is a landscape designed for an individual to which visitors are now admitted. When it changed from a private landscape to a public one, I insisted, and they have always agreed, that the paths should not be widened, that the scale should still be geared to the individual. If you are designing a public park, you have got to have wide paths because you know that crowds are going to use them, but if you are designing for an individual, you design for a limited number of people; the time-scale has changed too, for a visit lasts only an hour, whereas an owner is there indefinitely. The widths of the paths were not altered and where you have to walk two abreast or one behind the other, you still have to do so and the visitors have been organised in such a way that no more than 15 people at a time are allowed to go round in a party. Then they are allowed to wander free in certain areas and are collected to go into the next area. I think this is absolutely vital from the technical point of view because otherwise you can destroy the very thing you are trying to achieve, which is, in fact, the exploration of the mind of one man. The whole of Sutton Place is Stanley Seeger's mind, put on to the ground and this is fascinating because it displays all the different facets of the mind of a very able and eclectic man. The site is also fairly unique in being the subject of an extensive management plan and ecological study, particularly in relation to the river, the lake, the woodlands and the agricultural lands. Very early on I could see that with a client like this, there was a possibility here not only for landscape design, but also for ecology and I proposed that Marian Thompson should draw up an ecological plan for the whole of the estate. This has been very successful and the result is a combination of what I call mathematical, geometrical man, in the form of oneself and biological or ecological man in the form of Marian Thompson and the two things are in complete harmony.

My wife did the whole of the flower planting; it was her last project and it still looks absolutely beautiful. When one gets a very large work like that running into millions of pounds, one has to appoint people who have the backing to carry it out. I was very fortunate in the architect appointed to do the whole work, Clarrie McDonald, who built up a staff for this job, and I was very happy when two students from the Thames Polytechnic, Hilary Shrive and Rick Rowbottom, joined us, mainly to help my wife on the planting side. They must have been there for something like a couple of years and they must have learnt a great deal from it. My experience is that a fully trained student can be extremely useful provided they are prepared to fall in with the requirements of the job and it provides the student with an experience that can't be obtained in the schools.

Simultaneously I was given a commission which was totally different philosophically and in every way from Sutton Place, because it was for a public park for the communistic council of Modena. Whereas Sutton Place had been a study in the individual subconscious, now one was faced with the collective subconscious and I went there for a couple of days to see if I could do the job.

I fell in love with this group of people whose language I didn't understand at all – I had to have an interpreter – and they fell in love with me and seemed to understand exactly what I wanted with regard to landscape and the subconscious, in a way that no council or committee of council in England could. I find it very interesting that one's present ideas are being interpreted more easily by people outside England; after all, Stanley Seeger at Sutton Place was an American with a Greek background. The Italians carried my ideas ever further, as Stanley Seeger had done at Sutton Place, pushing me further into ideas than I would normally dare to go.

To carry out the work in Modena, I again went to Thames Polytechnic, and Harriet Phillips (she is married now with an Italian name) went out there and did absolutely brilliant work. Her training both here and in America meant that she could tackle that immense job, again running into a couple of million pounds, in a way that no one in Italy apparently could do. She remained on the staff of the commune about a couple of years and then she set up on her own, but she remained as advisor to the work, but unfortunately after about five years, the work ran into political difficulties. A great deal of it has been done: the long canal has been cut, the mountains have been more or less made, so I left them fully developed plans showing exactly what to do, as with Sutton Place. In view of one's age, one has done complete drawings so that one's intentions can be seen projecting themselves into the future. Technically I am still retained as consultant, on a retaining fee basis, which was much more than I deserved because I didn't have to do very much. The rule is that my scheme is to be carried out according to my plans and, as far as I know, that is happening now, but the political situation means that all the people that I met on my first visit have changed, all except for the Mayor who remains loyal to me, and his term of office will expire soon.

In 1983 the same eminent town planner who had asked me to do the Modena scheme, invited me to design another one at Brescia. Again I went out for a couple of nights and I produced what I think is a stunning scheme. They apparently liked it very much and I heard that they were implementing it, but I've heard nothing since. I had letters from the town planners saying there were political troubles so I don't know whether it will ever be done, but I have a suspicion that it will not be and I won't hear anything further. Again my drawings were such that they could be completed without me ever going to the site again, provided that they had an intelligent landscape architect to interpret the drawings.

Meanwhile, a botanist spending six months studying at Kew, financed by an American foundation called The Moody Foundation, was authorised by the Foundation to lay out a botanical garden in Texas costing many millions of pounds, and after visiting Sutton Place he wanted me to design it. As I didn't know anything about botanical gardens and I didn't really want to work in Texas, I declined his offer, but he was so persistent that after about six months of refusing I agreed in 1984 to go out and see the site. This was unlike any previous sites I had ever done

– it was appalling but it suddenly occurred to me that this was a challenge to the powers of a landscape architect: a chance to turn an utterly unfruitful barren landscape into something really worthwhile.

My terms of reference were fairly broad, that is to design a botanical garden on the required scale, but although the Foundation was prepared for a capital sum of up to 30 million dollars, it had wanted it to be self-supporting. They calculated that the upkeep would be about a million and a half dollars a year and the money would have to be raised by attracting visitors and since botanical gardens as such don't attract visitors, I had to make it attractive enough to ensure that it did. They sent me to Disneyland in Florida, which I was reluctant to do, but I was very glad that they did, because the landscape techniques are absolutely brilliant, how to handle fountains and all sorts of things like that which I had never before envisaged; one could incorporate what I call 'the fun and games' into the botanical gardens.

I sent them a scheme and nothing happened for a year, although I knew in any case that they would take a long time to consider it. Then they went cold on it, because they feared that my scheme would not attract enough people. It was a very grand scheme, certainly the grandest I have ever done in my life, but in their opinion it was too austere to attract the necessary number of visitors, so I was asked to do another scheme. Again I refused and again they were very persuasive. I felt that basically they understood what I was trying to do in attempting to provide a scheme that the pure landscape architect couldn't provide, and I felt sympathetic towards them, and it became a challenge. So I went out to Seattle, about 2000 miles away from the actual site,

Model of Harvey's roof garden, Guildford High Street 1957, recently closed to the public.

where they had collected a group of people, including exhibition designers who were involved with the Marine Esplanade at Liverpool, and we got round the table and evolved a totally new scheme with a totally different philosophy. I don't think it is so grand or splendid as the first scheme, but nevertheless it is much richer in human interest, which is what they felt would attract visitors on a very large scale, not only from Texas but from all over America. The scheme was accepted by the Foundation in 1985.

The first terms of reference were for the botanical garden, and I was very interested in the possibility of tracing the subject back through our own eighteenth century landscape romanticism, through seventeenth century English classicism, right back to Rome and to the Augustan poets. Virgil was the poet who inspired one for Modena, Ovid's *Metamorphoses* was my inspiration for Brescia and then I turned to a third poet, whom I admired tremendously. Lucretius wrote the greatest didactic poem ever written on the creation of the world *De Rerum Natura* and so when I was invited to do this work at Galveston on a pure botanical garden, I said at once that I would design a landscape which is like a poem of Lucretius. It relates man to the grandeur of the cosmos which is all about us, of which we are probably unaware in our daily lives, and I wanted to make people aware. That was too much for the Moody Foundation, who then wanted to include in the scheme a history of gardens. As it happens, I don't believe you can transpose gardens in this way: lots of exhibitions have had these Chinese and English gardens and so forth and because of their awkwardness in relating to a strange environment they just don't work. Again, they were very persistent so finally I got over my conscience by describing it as 'A History of the Plant in Civilisation, East and West' which is something quite different from the history of gardens, which is man's work, how man has used the plant. The resulting scheme is very involved because the site is so extraordinary, being subject to tides 12 feet high, to tornadoes and winds and all these have to be dealt with by protective dykes and barriers and goodness knows what, and from that has emerged the shape into which I have fitted the history of landscape. The whole thing is about a mile long and is approached by boat with water-buses running round the whole of the scheme, and then you have a complex of glasshouses 80 or 90 feet high, education centres, where you have the theatre, to explain what all the botanical side is about. What we are trying to do is to build up a collection of photographs of existing art to show how near, at any rate in essence, is this scheme that I have done to the real history of gardens – I show about 15 different landscapes, classical and romantic.

The Future
of Landscape Architecture

Susan and I have also been working as consultant editors on *The Oxford Companion to Gardens* which is concerned mainly with history. The executive editors, Michael Lancaster and Patrick Goode, have taken most of the responsibility and our job has mainly been to see that things are kept in balance – a gigantic problem really, keeping a balance between all the parts of this incredibly complex subject. It is not of course creative and in this respect contrasts with the *Guelph Lectures* published in 1983 by Guelph University in Canada, where one can say one has written one's philosophy of life and of the future of the profession.

I have a perfectly clear philosophy now in one's old age, that one can do good through one's work, which means that through this I should like everybody to experience life at a much deeper level than that of the visible world. It is greater than the nuclear bomb, for example, and if you get this feeling that you are related to the intangible aspects of the cosmos, then I feel it enables you to see everything in perspective. I think the raison d'être of the profession lies not only in good planning, and in making delightful scenes with water and so forth, but in creating an inner world as with any work of art. This is why I think the future of one's own profession is so tremendous. I don't think we have touched the fringe of what the landscape architect is going to do in the next few hundred years; western civilisation is only 'scratching the surface' and there is still the whole of the third world to be developed. I think it is this concept which no other art, not even architecture, can comprehend, that of the surface of the earth being ordered and seemly, affecting people's lives in the way that I have suggested, attempting on the very small scale within one's grasp to show people that there is something which transcends life. After all it has been done before by the Greeks, who gave the whole landscape a sense of the divine, of grandeur beyond this life. I see no reason why the ultimate aim of our civilisation – and I am talking about hundreds of years ahead – shouldn't be the same as for the Greeks, whereby we can sustain misfortunes with a deep philosophy that life is much more than its visible earthly semblance.

I think the job of the landscape architect is to help just by doing his work well, not commercially, but for the good of all. Every bit of good landscape helps towards this end and helps towards the objective of people living in harmony one with the other; whether Russian, American or South African, landscape offers real hope for the future.

Dame Sylvia Crowe

Born in Banbury in 1901, the daughter of Eyre Crowe, Dame Sylvia trained at Swanley Horticultural College and has spent most of her life in private practice and as consultant to public authorities, such as the Forestry Commission (1964 to 76). She was secretary of the International Federation of Landscape Architects from 1948 to 1959, president of the Landscape Institute 1957 to 59, chairman of the Tree Council 1974 to 76. Dame Sylvia has honorary degrees from the universities of Newcastle, Heriot-Watt and Sussex; she was awarded the CBE in 1967 and made DBE in 1973.

Early Life

Both my parents were devoted to the countryside which I am sure has had a great influence on me. My father was restless and was always wanting to travel somewhere where he hoped his health would be better. This meant as a very small child I travelled to France and Corsica and, even today, I can remember my fourth birthday in a Corsican forest sitting revelling in the carpet of wild cyclamen. So my appreciation of the landscape must have started very young indeed.

Originally my father was an engineer, but he retired comparatively early and I was a fairly late comer, so by the time I remember him he was retired from his original profession. Later he settled down as a fruit farmer and we had a fruit farm in Sussex. This was just before and during the first war. It was in the most delightful piece of country near a village called Felbridge, and the farm went down to the shores of a lake. It was very beautiful with a wonderful amount of wildlife and birds.

When I was 11 or 12 years old, I developed a form of TB which was taken very seriously in those days, so the doctor said I must not go to school. The result was that I had rather spasmodic lessons at home and spent most of the time wandering in the countryside and working on the farm. This was particularly necessary, because it was during the first war, when all the men had gone, and I therefore took on a great deal of work. At 14 or 15 I was looking after the small herd of cows, getting up at half past five in the morning, driving them down, milking, making hay and so on. From the educational point of view I was put at rather a disadvantage but in other ways it really was an advantage, because it meant that I was imbued with countryside values and an intense love of landscape.

My mother loved the countryside too, was a great walker and loved gardening, so I had sympathetic parents in that respect, on both sides. She used to describe her father as coming from a Midland yeoman family, whereas my father's family was more academic and a bit more artistic.

As a child, I bicycled over to William Robinson's Gravetye Manor. He used to open the garden before and during the war and I am sure his garden made a tremendous impression on me. I didn't see any of Gertrude Jekyll's gardens, but later on I knew about her and read her books. I think in my early life Robinson was a much greater influence just because I grew up with his gardens. So it was that style that appealed to me, in particular the sculptural feel, using the plants in a sculptural way. His informality had composition. My knowledge of plants was not too bad – the education on it at Swanley was quite good – and I was always interested in plants. When I was a child I had my own little garden. I always liked growing things, but I was more interested in the look of them than in their cultural requirements.

Professional Training and Influences

When the war ended I went to Swanley Horticultural College. In those days there was nothing as tiresome as an entrance exam – it was just an interview and if you seemed not too much of an imbecile, they would take you on. My idea at that time was to try to carry on my father's occupation as a fruit farmer. Earlier, curiously enough, somebody had put an idea into my head, when I was quite small, about designing gardens. I think at the age of seven somebody asked what I was going to do when I grew up and I said I was going to design gardens. Then the first war rather drove that idea from my mind and replaced it with the practical thought of fruit farming, so I went to Swanley with that idea and joined the course for two years. At the end of that time I took a job in a big garden looking after prize fruit for Colonel Lucas at Hobland Hall, near Gorleston.

Then I had a break – my parents got on the move again to France and Italy. I joined them on the Italian coast for the winter and had a few rather aimless years, but I did see places such as Florence and Venice and the Italian countryside, which made a lasting impression on me, and was more and more drawn back to the idea of designing gardens. At that time there was no course on this subject and there were really only two practitioners; one was Thomas Mawson, up in the north, and the other Edward White in London. Edward White had a large, long-established practice dealing mostly with private estates and large gardens and I went to him as a pupil in his London office, but for financial reasons was only there for quite a short time.

From Edward White I acquired some skills in how to survey or draw a site, although I don't think that he influenced my ideas on design much. I liked drawing at school but have never been very skilful at it. My father was a good draughtsman and good at watercolours and as a child I used to sketch when he was sketching, out in the countryside. I think the sketches were pretty bad but I enjoyed it immensely and it helped me to learn to see. For the gardens I designed, I drew mainly plans, sometimes sketches but not so often. Occasionally, I did models and got rather keen on contoured gardens, which were new in those days. I used to make plasticine models of these. I preferred informal gardens to the more formal designs of people like Mawson and Sudell.

Next I got a post as a garden designer with Cutbush, a firm who laid out gardens. For many years, until the outbreak of the second world war, I was with them designing gardens, mostly rather uninspiring suburban plots. Just occasionally there would be something a little larger and a bit more interesting. But it was very good training, because the firm had to carry out work which you designed and also you had to design in a small space. You couldn't smudge anything; you had to think of every square foot.

I think that my ideas of what a garden should be were absorbed from the things that I saw, books, pictures, but most of all from gardens and the landscape I lived in. At Cutbush I was lucky to work with Shirley Wainwright, who was editor of *The Studio*. He had a very strong design sense and I feel I owe him a great debt, because he was a fairly ruthless critic of my work. But otherwise, I had to find my own way and I probably did some things which were pretty awful and perhaps other things were rather better. At that time, too, we used to exhibit at Chelsea and for several years I designed one of the Chelsea gardens, one of which got a gold medal. This, I think, was in 1937. It was an informal, contoured garden and had a bluebell wood, from which flowed a stream into a pond. People then were inclined to make pools which showed the concrete edge and I devised a way by which the edge stepped down so that you could not see the concrete; the water lapped up to the shore, which, as far as I know, was then a new idea. I very audaciously designed a concrete summer house for the Chelsea exhibit and when it came to the techniques of it, I went to the Cement and Concrete Association. They were tremendously helpful and were thrilled that anyone was going to show a concrete summer house at Chelsea, so they bent over backwards to give me all the help they could. When it was built, however, it aroused great controversy among the Royal Horticultural Society die-hards, who disapproved of concrete in a garden. I was standing in the garden, almost on the point of suicide, when along came Geoffrey Jellicoe and lifted my sagging spirits by giving it praise. I was really grateful and it put everything right. Jellicoe was one of the first landscape architects I met and that was the start of a lasting friendship, although I already knew him through the Institute of Landscape Architects.

The only garden I have been back to was one I did up near Mold in Flintshire. I went back there just after the war to see how it was getting on. Some of it had come on quite nicely, but of other bits I thought 'I shouldn't have done that'. I think it's very rare that you look at a thing and are completely satisfied with it, particularly if it is the kind of garden that depends on plant growth, because you can't be sure that what you put in was right. But by and large I was contented.

Early Years of the ILA

I was a very early member of the ILA but I was not one of the group of founder members who met in the tent at Chelsea in 1928 although I came in very soon afterwards. The idea of developing a profession that could do more than garden design was in all our minds.

There was great concern about what was happening to the landscape at that time, for instance new roads were being constructed and we wanted them done properly. Some were planted by amateurs which was not the answer; we thought more should be done using professional skills. I think we were very sure of ourselves and we certainly thought we were something more than designers of gardens; there was no question whatever about that. We realised that different types of problems now existed. So many things were going on in the countryside such as roads, mineral workings and buildings and to absorb them the whole of the landscape and the whole of the city needed attention. Clough Williams-Ellis wrote two books, *Beauty and the Beast,* and *England and the Octopus,* and these were compilations by a wide variety of people who showed concern about what was happening to the English landscape; people like V.S. Pritchett, C.E.M. Joad, philosophers and in fact the intelligentsia of the time, seemed very concerned.

We had influential people from allied professions, like Patrick Abercrombie, who was a great supporter of the Institute and Thomas Sharp, Lord Holford and Lord Reith, who also gave great support – people from allied professions who realised we had a contribution to make, something to marry in to their work. There was a missionary optimism mingled with anxiety that you could not overcome the destruction and invasion of the English countryside in time.

The other problem then was the industrial landscape. I think we were aware of it, but maybe it was something which it was almost impossible to tackle at that moment. The important thing was to prevent further damage and to start rescuing the landscape which had already gone wrong. Since then there has been tremendous work on reclamation.

The first large-scale involvement of landscape architects in housing was in the new towns. Patrick Abercrombie who came to Council meetings before and during the war, was a major influence. He was vital in every way. There was a man who did things! He had ideas and purpose and he was far-seeing and a most attractive character. I think supporting the ILA was part of the breadth of his outlook. Abercrombie was a big enough man to see the picture as a whole whereas a lesser man could not.

At first we got little support from other professional bodies. The Royal Institute of British Architects (RIBA) thought that we should be absorbed within their orbit, but Brenda Colvin and I stood out and insisted we should be independent. That was a vital decision for the Institute to make and not an easy one, especially as most of our members were architects and/or town planners and to get them to realise that landscape architecture was a third different profession was not always easy. At the end of the war Scandinavia was our great inspiration, even though Norway and Denmark had been occupied. When we went to Denmark and saw the standard of landscaping relative to housing, we were inspired and also ashamed of the paucity of landscape work in our own country.

The War Years

During the second world war I served with both the First Aid Nursing Yeomanry (FANY) and the Auxiliary Territorial Service (ATS) as a driver. Fortunately, I had very early demobilisation due to great age and length of service. However, I think perhaps my experiences during the war strengthened the conviction that things needed doing; we all thought we could make a new world. I was not a born soldier and it was not the kind of life which I would choose, so that my desire to get back to more creative things and to landscape work was very great indeed. But it opened up to me an understanding of other people's points of view.

One of my happier memories was of the ILA Council meetings which, thanks to Geoffrey Jellicoe, kept going. When I could get a day's leave from the south coast where I was stationed, I went to the Council meetings. That was marvellous, because one got away from the grind of seeing things through and thought about the future. One's creative energies had had a stopper put on them and they came bubbling up; one had a longing to do something. I was a one-stripe corporal at the time and Lord Reith used to come in his Admiral's uniform but we all got together to think of the future. It was towards the end of the war, when the New Town idea came up and was talked about, that Lord Reith said there must be a section on 'landscape' in his report. He looked me straight in the eye and said 'you had better write it'.

Lord Reith had a very commanding presence; I think you always listened to what he said. He gave me the feeling that he was an utterly genuine man. Whatever he said he would do he did, and whatever he expressed interest in was genuine. I admired tremendously the fact that whatever his duties were as an Admiral, he took the time to consider the problems of this small struggling Institute.

Apart from Geoffrey Jellicoe, Brenda Colvin was also on Council then. She was a marvellous leader and her influence can't be overestimated. She had both vision and steadfastness of purpose and would never give up anything as hopeless if she thought it was the right thing. She was absolutely first class. Then there was Jackie Tyrwhitt: she used to rush in, drop a few bombshells, then rush out again, but she was a livewire; and there was Lady Allen of Hurtwood, who was a great person with tremendous drive and power. There were many issues to discuss but on the whole we agreed much more than we argued. We had a very good secretary called Gwen Browne, who kept us all together. James Adams too was a regular attender at our meetings. I remember he gave me great encouragement once. I was stationed at Gravesend, of all places, and took a long walk along the Thames and I thought 'wouldn't it be marvellous to have a walkway all along the Thames Estuary?' So I wrote it up and very bashfully sent it to James

Adams and he was so encouraging − saying that this was just the kind of thing we wanted to think about as soon as the war was over. You remember people who encourage you like that − it gives you confidence to look ahead. But there never has been a Thameside Park.

Post-War Opportunities

I was able to start work again, thanks to Brenda Colvin and Geoffrey Jellicoe. Brenda offered me house-room in her office in Baker Street and Geoffrey Jellicoe pushed work to me and with the help of these two I was able to start in a very precarious way; and from that I gradually built up a reasonable practice.

I worked on some small landscape projects for a few years before getting the consultancy at the start of the two new towns of Basildon and Harlow around '47 and '48. The biggest job passed on to me by Geoffrey Jellicoe was the reclamation of the sand dunes at Mablethorpe, which had got wrecked during the war because of gun emplacements. The wind was blowing the sand away and I had the very interesting work of finding out how to stabilise sand dunes. I visited Holkham estate in Norfolk, where they gave me good advice and I went about and saw what could be done and applied their technique to the dunes. Subsequently I made seaside gardens within the dunes.

Then Frederick Gibberd, who was the architect/planner of Harlow New Town, brought me in as consultant. I came in at the beginning and was able to do a landscape survey. I plotted every tree in the area and wrote a report on open space and treatment of the woodlands and so on. But it was really Gibberd's concept, because he did the master plan and he had the idea of open space and landscape flowing between compact housing areas. He had a great feeling for the landscape, so that I was wholly in sympathy with him and was able to work with that idea.

In the case of Harlow, I felt the character of the little woodlands and river valley was being kept and that there was going to be a flowing landscape up to the centre of the town. In the case of Basildon, it was a pretty grim landscape anyway, because it was a heavy waterlogged clay scattered with derelict bungalows and heaps of rubbish: anything we did there would be for the better. I was also in favour of open fronts for housing landscape, which certainly gave a pleasant feeling of continuity to the roads and landscape, but I think it is debatable whether, from the all-round view of the inhabitants, it was the right solution. But anyway, I was able to do a lot of new tree planting which gave a framework to the buildings; this was the biggest contribution I was able to make.

At Harlow we had a bit of marshy land by the river, meadow near the town centre and a lot of woodland. I think one can always go back and think 'I wish I had done that better'. I don't regret not having had beds of flowers; I don't think it would have gone with the general concept, nor have been practical from an upkeep point of view. One had to be very conscious of costs. Bearing that in mind, I think the general concept was a reasonable solution.

I haven't been back for several years. The last time I went, by and large, I thought the balance was pretty good.

As far as I know, Harlow was the pioneer in using all the foundation material for creative purposes. I happened to overhear a conversation between one of the planners and the engineers, who were saying they had so many cubic yards of foundation material which they were having to transport down the Thames and get rid of. So I said 'Do you mean you have all this spare quantity of material? Because if so, I would like some to build hills with.' So we made quite a range of hills between the housing and the industrial area. The same was done at Basildon. After I had given up being a consultant at Harlow, Mary Mitchell built a hill for skiing out of spare soil. That is something which one would normally think of now but there is always a first time. We were all aware of the social and recreational needs and one of my first projects at Harlow was a children's playground in a gravel pit. Bodfan Gruffydd designed the town park when he was a full-time landscape architect there. I think one is always learning from mistakes all one's life and I am sure we made some in Harlow, but there was throughout, by Gibberd, by White, the social development officer, and myself, a very keen realisation that one must cater for people's outdoor, as well as indoor life.

There was a tradition to bury water in town planning before this time and to put streams in culverts. We took special care to ensure

Sand dune reclamation at Mablethorpe.

that the stream at Harlow was not covered over and that it would have a park setting. In looking after what was there and making the most of it, the best that could be done was done. In the making of new features, woods were extended and water features designed. More might have been done, but in the New Towns we were fighting to keep costs down; it wasn't so much lack of vision as lack of resources. It's an inevitable financial problem. Now money is short – it was shorter then. We were recovering from the cost of war and the first priority was to re-house the bombed-out; it was a question of resource allocation. One might have, on one side, say, the desire for an indoor sports hall as against doing something outside. It was very difficult to say which was more important.

Formation of the International Federation of Landscape Architects

IFLA was born when the ILA decided to invite other countries to a conference and exhibition in 1948. A prime mover was Lady Allen. There was tremendous response from Europe and the Scandinavians were very active. They came over and we had meetings in London together with an exhibition of landscape work which made a great impression on people, including Lord Silkin, the Minister concerned with planning. We then went on to Cambridge to continue our international meeting. The delegates from different countries all said 'we have got to have an International Federation of Landscape Architects', and so it was founded at Jesus College, Cambridge and Geoffrey Jellicoe was elected president.

The enthusiasm was very strong, particularly among the Scandinavians, the Swiss and the Belgians. The Americans held back rather surprisingly: possibly because their own professional organisation (ASLA) was so large that they felt sufficient unto themselves – they joined later; Holland, France, Spain and Italy came in. The Spanish invited us to our first international meeting there in 1953, even though we were not on political speaking terms. It was a great success and from the landscape point of view, a very important step forward. The Festival of Britain in 1951 was another big step forward for the landscape world with the involvement of landscape architects Frank Clark, Peter Youngman and Peter Shepheard particularly.

I was influenced by the work of some of the Scandinavians, by Blom and Jakobsen and Sven Hansen. They all thought they owed a debt to Gertrude Jekyll and her concepts of planting, more, I think, than to the English parkland. Soon after that, when we visited Scandinavia, the thing that struck us was the skill of the planting, the use they made of foliage textures and the planting form. The private gardens were marvellous – mostly very small and again they had this wonderful knack of getting the forms right – they used rocks and boulders in just the right way as sculptural features. We found great inspiration there.

The Landscape of Power

The power station at Trawsfynydd, as I recall, was the first major battle between the conservationists and the Electricity Board. It was the first major attempt to build in a national park and to test the concept of the national park. I took no part in the inquiry. When Lord Holford, as the advisor to the Central Electricity Generating Board, rang me up and asked me to be Landscape Consultant in 1948, I said that if it were decided to have a power station there, I would be glad to , but wouldn't give evidence in favour of having it in a national park. He said 'if it does have to be there, I'd like you to do the best you can for it.'

The principle I went on was that you couldn't possibly mask the building they had there. It was much too big. It was a good building – they had Basil Spence as architect, but if I could civilise or conceal all the clutter that comes around these buildings, that was probably the best I could do. Before I started to do anything I went down to stay there and climbed all the surrounding hills – and they were real climbs. I couldn't do it now. But wherever you could look down on the site I went and I looked. I found, for instance, that where the sub-station was going to be was in full view from Rheinog. I haven't been back to see if it worked, but I got them to put white clover and fescue in the stone chippings on the floor of the sub-station. The engineers were worried I was going to cause an electric short! And then again, there was quite a bit of surplus soil so I made a hill range which cut off quite a lot of the view of the sub-station. Then I got them to sink the pump-house and I persuaded them not to have any lighting or kerbs on the approach road. They said 'we must have road lighting'. But I said 'won't the lorries have head-lamps?', and they said 'yes, I suppose they will'. For the approach road I was influenced by the landscape, that was the shape the landscape wanted. Then there had to be fencing, I didn't want the usual security fence, and Ian Purdy, who was with the CEGB, designed a new type of security fence that would be flexible and go up and down slopes and take curves. Then, together we chose a paint colour that would merge into the background – so it was quite unobtrusive.

There is an existing wood and it seemed quite reasonable to extend the general wooded feeling, and I thought the sub-station would be much less obvious against a wooded background. It is mixed woodland, but is intended to be predominantly hardwood; the conifers are mainly a nurse crop. I must go back in a few years time to have a look. It is one of the dilemmas in design to know whether to establish a woodland where no woodland exists, but I think one must remember in this argument that most of Britain was once wooded, so one is putting back what used to be there, which seems permissible unless you are blocking a view. The desire for the texture of open moorland is very strong as well, but it's not a good background for a thing like a sub-station, which is a cat's cradle of wires. I think that a solid cushioning background would absorb it better than a rock-strewn hillside. That was my idea. Basically I was concerned with creating a good setting – a form of camouflage.

From that I went on to Wylfa Head Power Station in Anglesey

and there built more hills. The problem there was that the sub-station had to be enclosed because of the sea air. The result was a gigantic boot-box. It was nothing else. Again I walked right along the coast from Amlwch to check all the points from which you could see it. Obviously the station couldn't be hidden but the boot-box could be – and hence the hill. (This point came up recently when someone from the CEGB said that hill was just a dump for subsoil – he hadn't a clue!) Later a 400kV cable would come right past the hills from the power station, but there was nothing I could do about it. The setting could have been so much finer if they could have put the lines underground for the last quarter of a mile, which is what I wanted them to do.

Books on Landscape Design

I think the first was *Tomorrow's Landscape* which dealt with a great many landscape problems with which I believe the profession had not had a great deal of experience then. It was based on thought and common sense and observation – wandering about and deciding on the relationship of one thing to another and how far you had to be away from something to bring it into scale with some natural object. I analysed this in *The Landscape of Power*, laying down the concept of zones and influence. I had fun doing that! I spent several weekends doing it by trial and error. Seeing how far back you had to be before something became insignificant or acceptable. It was very interesting and I enjoyed doing it.

I think 'change' was the subject I was dealing with. I was entirely in sympathy with the preservation of the countryside, but that was a point that had been got across – it had been said. What I was after was a really new approach; there must be change so what do we do about it? It would have been a longer book in two parts if I had dealt also with preservation.

However, why *does* one write books? I had thought a lot about it and had all these ideas. Sir Frank Layfield Q.C. was my neighbour then and he said, 'Sylvia, you must write a book about it'. So I spent my weekends writing books. When you write a book you always hope that somebody will be influenced by it but I didn't do it as a deliberate exercise in propaganda – it was just an argument I wanted to put forward. One of the points I made was that the future well-being of the land does mean you have got to keep the full range of species and plant life going. I think the book covered it but if I was writing it now, I would probably want to labour the point a bit more, because the dangers have increased since I wrote that. There are too many people who think only of adding that last ounce of cereal to the mountain and another pint of milk to the lake, instead of thinking of the welfare and beauty of the countryside.

There are parts of the countryside where in the last 10 years, the scale or rate of change to the farm landscape has been rather alarming. I think some of the East Midlands looks very bleak – Cambridgeshire and Bedfordshire. When you get right on to the coast I don't think there were many hedges – it was open to the wind. But when you get this prairie far inland, it is depressing.

The landscape profession has got something to offer the future of the farm landscape. With the sympathetic and knowledgeable cooperation of the agricultural people, we ought to be able to do something.

In some cases, it's just the acceptance of general principles. I came across one young man in the Countryside Commission, who is basically an agriculturalist – not a landscape architect. He was telling me that in running some model farms (demonstration farms) he found, here and there, a farmer who was sympathetic and had the right ideas, and he encouraged him to make the farm efficient and yet keep a reasonable proportion of hedges and trees. By encouraging these specimen farms, he could show other farmers how they could be both efficient and look after the countryside. I think that is the right approach. You've got to have someone who understands agriculture so I think one thing our profession needs to do is to get more contact with the agricultural profession – through mutual education perhaps. Some aspects of landscape design – landscape appreciation perhaps – could be taught in agricultural college and equally, a certain amount of agriculture should be taught to our students.

Garden History

I think it is basic to the landscape architect's design ability that he understands the interplay between the way of life and thoughts of a particular age, and the way this was expressed in a garden. From that we realise that the same thing has got to happen today; that the garden is a translation of the thought and way of life of a particular period. I think if one is interested in the subject one automatically finds out about the people who designed them, lived in them and used them. The best gardens of the past were a good reflection of the landscape designer's rapport with his client. We have today to do just the same thing – to understand what people want and translate their real needs; for sometimes people think they want something, but if you go into it more deeply you find that what they really want is something a little more subtle. We have to find out the *true* needs of the client and then try to meet them.

Stowe, Vaux-le-Vicomte and Villa Lante were all good results of what the clients wanted both physically and as a translation of their state of mind. For instance, the people who wanted Stowe and other landscape places like it, had a tremendous breadth of vision – a feeling of freedom, of the countryside. The best gardens all translate thought. They were given form and character by the landscape architect's own imagination and inspiration, but on the other hand, a lot of people, particularly in the 18th century, were pretty enlightened in the sense that they knew what they wanted. I would think in most cases that the designers of these places were comprehensive landscape architects in that they knew about planting, construction and engineering, but in some cases there would be collaboration between someone who perhaps designed the garden and someone else who was an expert on plants; but by and large they understood the whole thing.

Great historic gardens certainly made a tremendous impression on me the first time I went and the impressions were intensified in subsequent visits. I wanted to go on looking, enjoying, being in the garden. Just looking at it from one viewpoint is only a very small facet of appreciation. One wants to be in it — to walk about. I enjoyed it most when I had more than one visit. If the first time someone who knew the garden well showed me around that was marvellous, for example at the Alhambra. Prieto Moreno[1] opened my eyes to things which I might have overlooked and not understood the meaning of, but then I would also want to go around by myself to look and to think. You can't give your sole attention to anything if someone is talking or waiting for your reaction. You have to have a direct contact. You should never hurry through a garden — that is absolutely fatal.

Design for town garden, Wexham Springs.

Some people might argue that gardens are a bit of an anachronism today and that there are too many historic gardens and it is difficult to keep them all in the present state. I think there may be some that are not in the very top class and if something has to go it must be these, though I hope there are very few we could say that about, and I think that the appreciation of gardens has grown enormously in the last decade, so I am very hopeful that there would be no financial problems in looking after the best of our gardens – certainly in this country. Of course the other thing is that we have to have the people who really understand how they should be kept up. There are endless problems where the garden was the design of one man, like Hidcote – there are very difficult design problems when such gardens are opened to thousands of people and I think this is something to which the profession should give very serious thought. Sissinghurst is an example.

There would be some gardens where they could only manage a certain number of people at perhaps certain times of the year; they could not be open to everybody all the time. If it involved the destruction of the garden, I think an owner would be absolutely justified in not opening to the public. If he could allow people to see it, without damage, then I think it would be the nice kind thing to do, to open it, as most of them do now – at least on occasion. I do not think you should allow people in all the time – indeed, I don't see why you should. One would hope that people with works of art would allow others occasional access to them. I think it is a fairly widespread view now that the garden as a work of art is comparable to the house as a piece of fine architecture. If you look at the numbers visiting National Trust gardens I think it shows that the recognition of the artistic value of gardens is pretty general.

I think one problem may be that the contents of the garden change more. If you have a room furnished in the style of a particular period, there it stays. This only applies to the very formal historic garden, like Hampton Court. Looking at gardens is now a national entertainment. Wherever you go, people are finding gardens to look at and are planning weekends looking at gardens. There are a lot of villages which arrange to have a weekend when all the gardens are open to the public: I think this is excellent.

Principles
of Park and Garden Design

In my book *Garden Design*, I touch on the idea of the oriental garden, which induces contemplation, peace and meditation. I think it is an aspect we are in danger of neglecting. There is a great deal of emphasis now on active sports. As well as that, we do have a need for contemplative places in our public parks. We ought to be giving a little bit more thought to contemplative places.

A nice sense of containment is important. If you have a garden like our English landscape style in a public park, you have quite a lot of open stretches of grass, big groups of trees. That is fine to walk about in, but you also want more intimate areas, small glades, where you can sit and contemplate. Water usually helps contemplation, and restful forms are important. You can get the effect in a quite formal garden, like the old Queen Anne formal garden, but you can also get it in some of the more wooded places, where you have an informally shaped small piece of glade. You must have a certain feeling of containment. The containment has got to be a shape that gives a feeling of rest, whether it is formal or informal.

I think that sculpture can play a very big part in this. If you can get the right sculpture, it helps create a more personal response to the surrounding landscape; so do buildings. Things like a summerhouse are for recreation as well as contemplation and this idea comes from the pavilions in Persian gardens. The important thing is to get the right proportion and relationship between buildings and landscape.

Forestry and the Landscape

Being appointed as landscape consultant to the Forestry Commission in 1964 was quite a challenge. Fortunately there were some members of the Commission who were very interested in the landscape and above all were interested in nature conservation, and by working with these people to start with, I got some ideas across on pilot schemes. But one had to use discretion and diplomacy in the early days until gradually good landscape became accepted within the Commission. I think there were always people in the Forestry Commission who cared about landscape as well as timber production and it was a case of making their voices heard a bit more clearly, and perhaps getting the ideas of landscape values into afforestation on an accepted, almost codified basis.

I think that aesthetic and ecological principles are inseparable, certainly in afforestation. If you have a forest that is ecologically good, it is almost sure to be visually good, except perhaps in the shape of the outline, which could be quite arbitrary; shape was one of the things one had to tackle. The purchase of land was done on a plan without any compromise and there was usually a strict boundary, drawn at headquarters (then in London) without any reference to the site. So one got these awful straight-edged forests – straight down the mountainside. There would be a problem – either they had to get a bit more land to alter the shape, or to give up a little bit and not plant it, which would have meant forgoing a certain amount of profit. This was one of the most difficult things to deal with but now the landscape is taken into account at the time of acquisition. Getting in from the beginning, as early as possible, is very important if landscape considerations are to influence the conveyancing of land for forestry – using natural rather than artificial boundaries.

I believe that the planting should be made to talk the same

language as the terrain. A hillside with a wavy line going up it could look as silly as a dead straight one, unless you get scree or rocky outcrops which give you a reason for breaking the planting line. Then again if the growing conditions were much better at the bottom of the hill than at the top, that was a reason for breaking out so that you got a kinder line, but never an arbitrary one. Leaving rocky outcrops exposed may seem rather 18th century picturesque, but it's quite practical really; trees won't grow well where there is rock, so you are using the peculiarities of the terrain – using the trees to express the terrain. I think that is the best way one can put it. It is the same for a mixture of hardwoods; the best land for the hardwoods is at the bottom of the hill and so one works some hardwoods in from the valley floor, taking advantage of any drifts of better soil. (If you have a sympathetic forester who knows his land he will say 'that is a good bit of land'; 'the larch will do quite nicely on that piece'.) Do not make it an absolute rigid outline; break one species into another. That, I admit, is entirely visual, but the general disposition of the planting is based on soil and exposure. We found often we had to compromise, on larch, for example, which was termed our 'honorary hardwood' because it had a timber value, whereas the true broadleaves on upland sites had little timber value. It was sheer conservation but yet you were prepared to give a bit for that. Sometimes beech was possible and that was marvellous.

The Forestry Commission has been criticised on the grounds that there is no reason why a national forestry organisation should not have, as its main objective, the maintenance of vegetation cover, wildlife and the conservation value of trees to the landscape, rather than the production of economic timber. I absolutely disagreed with the pure monetary policy – but it was not primarily the fault of the Forestry Commission but of the Treasury, who were breathing down their necks, saying that they had got to make it pay. The Treasury was our common enemy. Originally the Forestry Commission was set up after the first world war to produce timber for needs of defence when the nation's lack of timber was revealed. That legacy may still be with us today, but I think that as a national policy it is wrong; it was understandable at the time and the devastation of timber again in the second world war showed there was some excuse.

The same principles should be applied to all areas. I think it is reasonable to expect a greater sacrifice of profit in the amenity and national park areas, but I do not think that the ecological and landscape side should be ignored, even in remote places; certainly not the ecological side, or even the visual side. More and more people are going to more and more unexpected places. Quite apart from who sees it, and when, the landscape has its own rights and it ought to be taken care of.

It has been argued that the use of conifers or non-native species was liable over the long term to deplete the value of the soil. This was a very difficult problem and many discussions were held about it. I wasn't dogmatic about it – I didn't know. A lot of foresters were very interested in the subject and it was thought there was a certain danger. As far as introduced species, as opposed to conifer, are concerned, that is another question again.

While I was with the Forestry Commission the *Nothofagus* was introduced. This seemed to me a good thing because it was deciduous and so presumably would give quite good soil improvement. It was first planted by Mr Best, conservator for the Forestry Commission in Wales, and I was very impressed by it. It grew very fast and was nicely formed with attractive foliage. I am not dogmatic about introduced species as long as they do not push out our natives! After all, few of our species are not introduced. The oak has more wild life on it than any other species and that is an argument for planting and keeping our older native trees, rather than an argument against ever bringing in a new species. One must balance it.

I know that the Forestry Commission is taking landscape more seriously now. As well as a consultant, they have their own landscape architects – I think they now have three – care for the landscape is obviously growing as they are getting more influential.

St Mary's churchyard, Banbury.

46

Landscape Planning

Landscape planning is a tremendously important element in the profession and I would like to think that there is a big future in it. There is a lot of international interest. There is an environmental planning committee (of which I am a founder member) in the International Union for Conservation of Nature and Natural Resources, and that has representatives from all over the world. When one goes to their meetings one realises how vital and difficult their problems are. At the last one I went to in Geneva, we discussed the problems of planning forests for conservation. There was a very interesting contribution from Zimbabwe – and there was a man from Egypt discussing the problem of reclaiming the desert. It is something which involves the whole world. We have misused so much of the land and it is the landscape planners' job to regenerate what has gone, as we can do with our industrial land, and to help guide developments so that they do not destroy the land and the landscape.

A lot of people who are concerned with the future of our forests, the growing problems of expanding deserts and the destruction of the countryside, are not landscape architects. I think we have something to contribute because we are in a position to see the thing as a whole; my experience with many of these specialists is that they are splendid at their own speciality, but they do not seem to see how one thing locks in with another. I remember some years ago when I was in India, and we were doing a project – somewhere north of Calcutta where all kinds of interesting things were combined – agriculture, fisheries, navigation, etc., and the people on the team were all splendid at their own particular speciality. As the only landscape architect it fell to me to put all these different elements together, to produce a plan to show how all these points could be combined. That was a very simple exercise, but I think it illustrates what the landscape planner should be able to do, to listen and understand what other experts have to say and combine them together into a viable whole. One must be aware that the other specialists will be seeing how the thing will work – but they will not be seeing how it is going to look. It is up to the landscape architect to put the whole thing together and say 'I think if this is done then we will have a good landscape'.

The Future for the Profession

I was working at the Liverpool Festival site in 1983/4 and as a result I am optimistic for the profession, because the Liverpool Festival itself will make people that much more interested in design. The fascinating thing was the enormous range of different interests and concerns, all the different countries – about 16 of them – making their gardens and that is bound to give a fillip to garden design. Liverpool is just the first; by the time this is published the second will have taken place in Stoke-on-Trent in 1986, so that the idea of designing landscapes has been given a great impetus.

These exhibitions are bringing the idea of plants and design together, the Royal Horticultural Society in particular is highly involved in the organisation. There have been many divisions between the professions during my career, but gradually we are overcoming this. There has been a great rapprochement between the architects and the landscape architects for some time. Now one gets, fortunately, counties and cities where the chief planner has appointed a landscape architect, so that the profession is given recognition. I think the horticultural side is rather slow still. They perhaps feel that we are encroaching on their territory, but I think that will be overcome too.

It is important for the future of the landscape that the right legislation is enacted. My own experience of the results of legislation has been through public enquiries, which have to take place before any major development in the countryside. Whoever is trying to do the development has to have a landscape witness and that can be very interesting. I think one of the biggest reservoirs I have dealt with was Rutland Water. There was tremendous opposition and there was a very long enquiry, but we won in the end and the reservoir went ahead. Having had me to give evidence, they were more or less in honour bound to have me give landscape advice on carrying it out. It was a very challenging undertaking to make a reservoir acceptable in the landscape. This has happened in quite a lot of cases; for instance the Central Electricity Generating Board. If it had not been for public enquiries these authorities might not have bothered to get professional advice. However, as a profession we must be very, very careful not to abuse this position. If you are asked to be a witness you must really believe in what you are giving evidence for. This is a moral issue and a very important one for the credibility of the profession, that people know we believe what we are saying; that we are not simply doing it because it will be a job for us.

Conclusion

Looking back on my career as a landscape architect, there are many events that come to mind, some of which have given me particular satisfaction. Going right back before the war, I was doing mostly private gardens and it was a tough life; there were one or two which gave me enormous pleasure, but I do not look at it as one of the most satisfying times of my life. After the end of the war I went into private practice; then new vistas opened up and I enjoyed tremendously a lot of the things I was doing.

Apart from the actual projects, I remember very clearly we had an International Exhibition at the time of the Festival of Britain. This was a very courageous thing to do, because we were a minute institute with no money and we sent out invitations to most of the European countries to come – this was absolutely splendid. Everyone thought it sheer effrontery, that such a small hard-up institute should stage an international conference at that particular time, and so everyone helped us – the LCC lent us County Hall, and the Duke of Wellington opened the exhibition for us as Lord Lieutenant of London, and ministers came and spoke to us, and so on – so it was a terrific success. We had a wonderful response from overseas – the foreigners particularly wanted to start an international federation, so we started that – at Cambridge; Geoffrey Jellicoe was elected as president and I was honorary secretary. The general secretary was René Pechère from Belgium and he and I worked in close liaison, constantly flying from one country to another. This grew and we had meetings all over the place – first of all Spain, which was at that time not diplomatically recognised, and they thought we were the first break of dawn and gave us a colossal reception. We went from country to country to these splendid meetings and now we have 30 member countries and so it really has been worthwhile. I have got as much of a kick from that as out of any of my professional activities.

Oxford University, Department of Educational Studies; part of the courtyard.

From a work point of view, the best thing was the Forestry Commission, in terms of both achievement and interest and, I think, in terms of the people I was working with too. The whole thing was to me very rewarding. Then there were the water authorities, with all the reservoirs, which I am still doing and that I enjoy very much too. I had a long session with the Central Electricity Generating Board, siting power lines, which was interesting, but about the most thankless work I have ever done, because wherever you put them somebody hates them, but on the whole I enjoyed it. I did quite a lot of work for the Oxford colleges – University College – again very nice people.

My involvement with the Landscape Institute was very exciting because again I saw the profession gradually growing and being accepted, and I remember the problems we had to get any course going in landscape architecture, whereas now they are flourishing. So there was a terrific feeling of struggle, but also a certain amount of achievement, and a wonderful feeling of friendship with those of us who were working together. I have very affectionate memories of the secretary, Gwen Browne, and Geoffrey Jellicoe and Brenda Colvin, who did such great work.

I went on a lecture tour of the States. I found that very interesting – very refreshing; I had a wonderful time; they showed me all kinds of things. Theirs was a huge profession compared with ours, but I still found in some ways that we had a broader outlook than

Oxford University, Department of Educational Studies; sculptural design feature with rocks and plants.

they had in the international sphere. I have a great admiration for the United States. I spent about a week at TVA[2] staying in the Smoky Mountains and looking at all the dams and reservoirs and the wonderful forests, and that was absolutely marvellous. Afterwards I went to an IUCN (International Union for Conservation of Nature and Natural Resources) meeting in the Rockies, and the American Forest Service took me on a trip in a tiny two-seater plane to show me how they did their felling – in small coups and nice shapes, so they are all swallowed up and regenerated. Then I stayed with a forest officer in the Rockies and he showed me, amongst other things, how he had made ski runs down the sides of his forests – not straight lines but interesting curves, which incidentally stopped the wind blowing up them. All that I found very interesting. The last time I went was to California, to Berkeley: where Michael Laurie is head of the Department of Landscape Architecture at the university. In his early professional days he was in my office and I have a high regard for his work. I also saw a lot of Thomas Church's gardens, small gardens which are absolutely superb. I think his book is marvellous. I went to lunch with Laurence Halprin and he showed me some of his work, including the Levi Piazza, full of fountains. I remember him on my first visit as a very young man; we ate sandwiches together on a windswept beach in San Francisco. At that time he was doing a hospital in Jerusalem, which I saw when we went on one of the IFLA tours of Palestine.

I have enjoyed being a landscape architect; I would not have wanted to be anything else. But you have got to be wholehearted about it, because no holds are barred and there are no water-tight compartments. It embraces so much, you have got to think about the human side, particularly when you are designing for towns, parks, and also, for instance, with these reservoirs. It is very largely the recreational side I have to worry about, because the water is there anyway. The dam's fine if you have a good engineer. Really nice engineers consult you, to ask about what type of dam would be best, Wimbleball, for example, is a beauty – a lovely dam. But what you largely have to deal with is the people who come there – and of course their cars; how are you going to prevent the cars from absolutely ruining the landscape.

The landscape architect has to understand what the people want and to understand what the wild life wants, as well as understanding the function of whatever it is you are undertaking. There is a great deal to think about...

Notes

1 Prieto Moreno is a distinguished Spanish landscape architect and historian who was in charge of the gardens at the Alhambra and wrote a book about them.
2 The Tennessee Valley Authority was established in the 1930s by the US government to replan a vast region which had become a dust bowl as a result of over-cropping (see also Hackett).

52

Sir Peter Shepheard

Sir Peter Shepheard has practised as architect, town planner and landscape architect. Since 1971 he has been Dean of the Graduate School of Fine Arts at the University of Pennsylvania. He has served on various bodies such as the Countryside Commission and the Royal Fine Art Commission and is Honorary Artistic Adviser to the Commonwealth War Graves Commission. Sir Peter was President of the ILA from 1965 to 1967 and of the RIBA from 1969 to 70. He was appointed CBE in 1972 and knighted in 1980.

Early Life and Influences

It all goes back to my interest in natural history, which is still my main love by far.

My father was an architect, the son of a farmer in the Midlands. As a boy he wanted to be an architect but he had no idea how to become one and he was apprenticed first to a builder in Cambridge. It took him some time to realise that that was not leading him in the right direction, and then he got some better advice and went to Manchester to be articled to an architect. And there he met Patrick Abercrombie and his brother Lascelles the poet. Pat Abercrombie then went to Liverpool as professor of City Planning at the University and persuaded my father to go there and take a job with Arnold Thornely. This was in Liverpool around 1900; he set up practice there in 1910 as Shepheard and Bower. His career started badly; quite soon the first world war wiped the practice out and as soon as they got going after the war the depression attacked them. He really made very little money in architecture but he was a wonderfully nice, gentle person. He and a number of other impecunious architects had a tiny little cottage in Birkenhead which was up a side lane in Oxton, not far from where Pat Abercrombie lived. The others left the cottage one by one; my father was the last one to get married and he carried on in this little broken down Victorian cottage. It was a charming place, with a sweet little garden buried up a pretty rustic lane in Birkenhead, which otherwise was not a very presentable place, a very rough ugly town.

I remember writing a thesis at school on the history of Birkenhead which interested me a great deal. The city fathers of Birkenhead had founded it ambitiously somewhere around 1830 to compete with Liverpool. They had a better side of the Mersey for shipping, they thought, with a useful inlet where they could make great docks and build a city. They sent the Town Council to Rome, of all places, to discover how to build Birkenhead and so they started off very well – great Georgian squares, where the owners could look over their docks and Paxton's park. And then it all went wrong because the tram, and later of course the motor car, were invented. The horse tram *began* in Birkenhead, first in the world, and loosened it up to become suburbs instead of this great compact Georgian town. The Georgian part was occupied quite soon after its inception by seamen and sailors and lascars, and Birkenhead park was surrounded at a very early stage by strange and slummy areas. I remember Birkenhead, its mixture of grandeur and slums, with affection.

We had very little money, but we had this charming little house and garden and I soon got a bicycle. Snowdon was only 70 miles away, so all through my school days and my university days I was tearing off to the countryside. When I left school I wanted to be a naturalist; my hero was Gilbert White. In fact I quite seriously thought that I might be a country parson – my uncle was a country parson – and I thought if you could be a Gilbert White and get a curate, you could spend your whole life studying nature in the countryside; this seemed to me ideal. This was when I was about 14, an age when most people think of being engine drivers. But a country parson naturalist was my ideal, and so my headmaster sent me, when I was about 17, to see a biologist who later became famous, C.B. Williams, who was an old boy of the school. He was, I suppose, about 20 years older than I but to me he looked as old as Methuselah; he lived in a kind of hermit's cave of a room at the top of a Victorian house, entirely surrounded by cases of mounted locusts on the wall. He said 'forget all this natural history business, science is serious stuff, you've got to *specialise'*. He suggested (I think) 'the diseases of the gut of the red locust, now there's a thing for your next 25 years, that would be a good job for you!' It seemed that the only way to live by natural science in those days was to become a biologist connected to the colonial service and go out to Africa for 25 years, come back with malaria and all kinds of other things, to perhaps run a country museum. The whole thing looked wrong to me.

It was very strange, because many years later I met people who had done it differently. I met, for example, James Fisher when I was 52, a man who had done exactly what I wanted; but he had been to see Julian Huxley when he was a young man instead of C.B. Williams, I must digress here in order to finish the story. Many years later, when I was president of the RIBA, we had an annual party and I thought what fun it would be to have the party with a landscape theme and invite all the naturalists. So at the reception we had Peter Scott, James Fisher, Julian Huxley, Fraser Darling and others – a really grand crowd of people. I was talking to them afterwards and they all said 'how did *you* get interested in this natural history business?' I told the story about C.B.

Williams, and they began to laugh. Apparently he became a world specialist on the migration of nocturnal moths – quite something as a specialisation. I said 'you know I've often thought that, wherever he is now, I probably know more about alpine plants, monkeys or fish than he does.' And they said, 'well of course you do, because he is absolutely a moth man, and that's it.' Fisher, whom I had met on the Countryside Commission deliberately called himself a naturalist, and believed that the 'superview' was the thing. He was right of course. He was the kind of man who learned Anglo-Saxon in order to find out what the gannet was doing in Scotland in the year 800, a wonderful man. Gilbert White was his hero too.

I went back to father and said 'I can't do this C.B. Williams thing, so I'll be an architect like you.' It felt like an enormous lapse into something easy. I could draw, and architecture felt like the line of least resistance. Father was half overjoyed and half thoroughly worried, I think. However, I went to Liverpool University. I had been aiming at Cambridge; I was trying to take a scholarship to do science, and there were only a few weeks to go. So I swatted like mad in the summer of that year and managed to take an exam which won me a scholarship to the Liverpool School of Architecture and had my fees paid. Then the RIBA gave me £100 (the RIBA scholarship) and I had another £100 from the Architects' Benevolent Society's Scholarship. So I had £200 per annum and my fees paid and all the time I was at the University my father earned £80 a year. It was really very extraordinary, because I was giving £100 to my mother for my keep and living quite a happy life. What was good about all that was of course that I learnt to work without having to think about money – that money was awful but necessary stuff and you must not spend too much time worrying about it. I was enormously grateful for this scholarship.

My mother and father were very helpful to me and loved providing me with pencils and paper to draw with. I drew mostly birds and plants. I don't remember my parents having a passionate interest in nature, but my father used to sort of follow up; later he got very interested in alpine plants. I think I really was very interested in the natural world right from the start. I remember one very important thing: my uncle Reg, my parson uncle, gave me for my thirteenth birthday, *Butterflies of the British Isles* by Edward South, in the Wayside and Woodland Series. I had already been getting these books out of the public library. The bird book *Wayside and Woodland Birds* I already knew, and my uncle spotted that whenever I went to the library, I came back with these books so he gave me one for my birthday. That was my first book; I feel about it as Gertrude Jekyll did at the same age – 13 – when somebody gave her the Rev. C.A. John's *Flowers of the Field* which she said was 'probably the most valuable present she ever received'; that's exactly how I felt about this book. I've still got it. So then of course I really began to be interested and started to collect butterflies in earnest.

We weren't really too badly off for nature. We were on the edge of Birkenhead in Oxton, and we could walk into the Wirral. In those days the Wirral was a marvellous resource; it has been absolutely ruined by speculative builders since then, but in those days there was Arrowe Park and the rest of that valley and its funny little stream and so on, and I had a bicycle so I could get across to North Wales as well. Long before I could even hold a pencil, I think my very first memory was of Birkenhead Park. I used to think my very first memory was my fifth birthday, armistice day of the first world war. I can remember my father coming home early and all the ship's sirens going off. We could hear them from our house. But, even before that, I remember feeding the ducks in Birkenhead Park. I think it must have been from my pram; I really don't know how old I was. We went there very often with my mother. My mother was a very lively curious girl who kept us all going. She very much liked the visits of Abercrombie, who lived across the hill and used to blow in at weekends and always had something interesting to say. Sir Patrick Abercrombie, as he was to become, was in fact my godfather.

One day when he was there, I remember he suggested a game. My mother loved walking to Birkenhead Park, or to anywhere else in Birkenhead. She was very interested in people and the way other people lived. There were incredible slums in Birkenhead. She liked walking in these slums and seeing how people got on. So Abercrombie suggested this marvellous game, which was to take a ruler and stand it up on the 6″ map of Birkenhead on our house, and let it fall, and draw a line along it, and then walk along the line, turning right and left all the time. That was a lovely idea. We had lots and lots of these walks which led to all kinds of places. And I think I got interested then in the way things were put together. There were the docks which were magnificent. And of course it was not only Birkenhead; there was Liverpool which was a very interesting, lively city and there was the river, and going over on the ferryboats. There was a tremendous amount of environmental pizazz around plus the perfectly gorgeous countryside of North Wales. I will never forget how much North Wales meant to me. I believe quite honestly that one learns one's attitudes in landscape and environmental design from the countryside before the age of 14. You learn them when you are a boy, when you've got a bicycle and you are going exploring, and North Wales was just gorgeous. It is still my favourite place. In Birkenhead there were two factions, there were the Lake District enthusiasts and the North Wales enthusiasts. I was irretrievably committed to North Wales; I thought the Lake District had been absolutely ruined by poets and literature and much worse things than that, like Hugh Walpole. You could actually see a signpost at Watendlath pointing to a tarn which was the scene of the murder in *Rogue Herries* – a really awful fictional character imposed on the landscape. But North Wales was rugged. It may be full of slate quarries but it is relatively unspoilt by false romance. I suppose I am very anti-romantic, perhaps that's it – reality is the thing. Talking about influences, I got a book out of the library by Gertrude Jekyll – *Wood and Garden.* I remember reading this book as an innocent child of 15, when we were making the garden. I was enthralled with it. She didn't die until 1934, but I never met her.

I lived in Birkenhead until I was 23, when I graduated from Liverpool, and then came to London. In that early part of my life the whole scene was Birkenhead, Liverpool, North Wales, the bicycle and the natural history. When I was about 13, I was keen to have a place to keep frogs, fish and newts and things. I kept badgering my father, 'couldn't we make a pond in the garden' because I knew somebody who had a little pond, and in the end my father decided that we could. So we dug up the whole of the bottom of the tiny garden and cast a little concrete pond ourselves, put pipes down to it from the water butt to make a fountain, and filled it with sticklebacks and rudd which we caught in the Wirral. Of course, digging out this pond gave us a great pile of soil. The pond was only 7' by 3' but you can get a lot of soil out of that and this soil was the beautiful sandy peaty soil of Birkenhead – wonderful stuff. They were then making the Mersey tunnel and my father had the idea that he would stop one of the trucks carrying the sandstone from the Mersey tunnel and get the driver to dump a load at the top of our lane.

So we built a small rock garden and I started getting interested in alpine plants and reading about them in books from the library. Farrer's book *The English Rock Garden* really started me off. I remember how I got it. My father met Mrs Rathbone (who had been a client of his) in a book shop in Liverpool. She was looking at Farrer's thick two-volume book (which in those days cost 5 guineas for the pair) and he said 'you know that is the one book that my son Peter would give his ears for'. Mrs Rathbone said 'take it to him from me', and she bought it there and then, and father brought it home for me. I hadn't spent a penny on books; all the others had come from the library and now I had this unbelievably wonderful book – I still use it almost every day. I think that his description of a rock garden did more than anything, except Jekyll, to tell me what garden design was all about. Rock gardens are now rather out of date, but his whole idea about the rock garden was aesthetic; it was the lines of it and the character. Both he and Jekyll, every time they talk about plants, are talking about art – they don't use the word, but it's an art all the same, especially Jekyll; consider chapter XVIII of *Wood and Garden* on the colours of flowers, or her description of the leaves of *Alchemilla alpina* in *Home and Garden*.

Early Career

Sir Charles Reilly was head of the School of Architecture for my first two years and then he retired and Professor Budden took over for the last three. So I knew Reilly quite well. Abercrombie was teaching Civic Design and I stayed on to take the planning course. I did enjoy it enormously; it was a wonderful time. I had a great rival, still a dear friend, Donald Reay, who is now in California, and he and I were competing for everything. He could draw wonderfully well, much better, I thought, than I could. In the end we both got into the finals of the Commonwealth Fellowships – it was the first time Liverpool had got into the finals for a long time – but he won it and I didn't. So he went to America and I stayed behind, intending to do the city planning course, but they awarded me, I suppose as a kind of consolation prize, the University scholarship, which was a very prestigious thing. The University scholarship was open to the whole University, not just the architects. They insisted that I should accept it because it was an honour for the School but it carried the condition that you had to do research and must not take a qualifying exam; so I couldn't take the town planning exams. But I took the course and had all Abercrombie's lectures and Dougill's lectures and so on, and for my research I wrote a thesis on gardens. This was really terribly lazy. It was largely based on a book by Gromort, *L'Art des Jardins*, which I found in the library, which was a history of gardens, an excellent book actually. I sort of rewrote that book as an essay, and that's all I did. Shameful really, because I didn't do much to justify the scholarship. But it gave me a year to think and intensified my garden mania.

There was little about landscape in the Liverpool course. I remember them giving us a building in a park as a design project. Most were content to draw a line around the park and paint it green, but I *designed* the park. I remember drawing all the trees in it and putting in the Latin names and being regarded as an absolute eccentric but getting a very good mark for it. But it really was uphill work. There were a number of lecturers who were quite interested in landscape. Gordon Stephenson, I remember; he was five years older than I and he had been to Russia so he was very glamorous to us. When he was young he was splendid. He had black hair and a red beard, and usually a red shirt as well, desperately trying to turn us all into young socialists, but we weren't ready for that. However, although there were a few others who were interested, I found you couldn't really learn anything about landscape from the way the School was set up. But I had my books, my Farrer and my Jekyll, and my rock garden.

I met Clough Williams-Ellis once or twice when I was a student. My father knew him, not well, but slightly. Of course I read his books, *England and the Octopus*, and others, very influential books. He was another hero; later on I got to know him better. I remember he came to see the Festival of Britain and was wonderfully supportive about that. One of the best things about him was that he was ready to be enthusiastic about other people's enthusiasm. So many architects are jealous of all other kinds of work except their own. I found him wonderful because he loved the Festival of Britain, which couldn't have been more unlike Portmeirion as a stylistic affair. But he loved the whole idea behind it and particularly the landscape.

Of course Abercrombie was a big influence. Liverpool was an extraordinary place. From 1900 onwards, it had been full of all sorts of people who were very interested in landscape and the arts; Abercrombie was part of all that. Then there were the Lake District people, and the artists. For example, my father was a founder member of the Sandon Studios Society, an artists' club which in its early days was the centre of a strong group of artists – including Augustus John for a time – who were working and teaching in Liverpool; it was a very lively artistic place and there was a growing tradition there. Abercrombie was of course intensely fond of the landscape. He had a natural sense of landscape and I think perhaps I have understated his influence upon me in that. I think he is the only true genius I have met; he really was quite out of the ordinary. He was immensely enthusiastic for all sorts of things. He would talk to my mother, who had little education, about all kinds of things. There was *nothing* he wasn't interested in as far as I could see. He was absolutely all-embracing in his enthusiasm and a wonderful talker. He had a very incisive high voice, which could be heard all over the place. If you talked to him in a restaurant everbody listened to what was going on at your table. He was thin, like a bird. He had a very sharp face. He always reminded me of a very alert member of the Corvidae: an elegant crow. He had black hair, which stayed black until he died, I think, and a rather red complexion, with a very bright piercing gaze. He only had one eye – there were various stories about it. My mother told me he lost an eye in a fit of coughing when he was a very young man, and there was another story about a firework; but as my father said, he saw far more with one eye than most people did with two.

He came from a very distinguished family. His brother Lascelles was a poet and there was another brother, a doctor. There was a very strong natural bent in Abercrombie to be interested in the world and the way it works and he had an absolute conviction that you could change it. He starts the little book he wrote about town planning with a sentence that says 'there are two kinds of men, those who accept their surroundings and those who try to alter them; of the latter are planners made'. It was possible to alter things; that was the key to his whole personality.

It was very much built into the Liverpool tradition, that architecture and planning and landscape were really one. I still stick to this. I remember years ago giving a talk about landscape and, quoting Clausewitz on war – 'war is an extension of politics by other means' – saying that landscape is simply an extension of architecture by other means. And the landscape architect, Michael Ellison, said 'Peter, you're wrong, architecture is an extension of landscape'. Of course he was right; landscape came first.

I remember when I first taught in America, in '59, at my first talk about landscape at the University of Pennsylvania, one of the students got up and said something about how lucky we were in England to have so much countryside left. I remember absolutely going off the deep end and saying 'Look, that's not luck, that was Patrick Abercrombie, Clough Williams-Ellis and a few other dedicated men who thought, years and years ago, that we could stop the English landscape being slaughtered. When I was a young man there were huge billboards all the way up the railway line from London to Liverpool. There were two huge wooden men carrying a ladder advertising paint and there was a big poster saying "only a hundred miles to Blackpool" – a hundred miles away out in the country. Just like America. And the fact that we got those all squashed wasn't luck; it was the absolute dedication of a few.' These young men said, 'well you know, it's obviously impossible here. How can we take on the advertising agencies and the developers?' And I said, 'that is the voice of the devil. If you really think you can't, then you can't,

OK, that's it. But don't forget that England looked like that , it was going the same way, and England is a fortieth of the size of the USA, so England was in much greater danger; the fact that the countryside is preserved now is almost entirely owed I think to those few people' – because Abercrombie put it into the Planning Act, via Holford (Sir William Holford). The '47 Planning Act turned planning from a negative into a positive thing. Instead of saying you must colour land green to preserve it, they said let us leave all the country land white and colour the land to be built on pink; now that was a revolution. That was nationalisation of the development right in land, without anyone knowing it had happened. I said to the students, 'look, if you young men have lost your guts about it, my prediction is that the women's garden clubs of America will do it for you. You'd better go out and find out what those girls are doing.' And there was a big laugh; but by God, ten years after that, in about '69 I think it was, the first move was made to ban advertising on the freeways, it was the garden clubs, not the architects who did that.

Career Development

When I graduated from Liverpool, Professor Budden wrote to Derek Bridgwater, who wanted someone for his office, and recommended that I should go and work for him. So before the war, I had three absolutely blissful years working in the office of Derek Bridgwater, whose partner I later became. When the war broke out, I joined the Propellant Planning Department of the Ministry of Supply (which was building ordnance factories, huge spread-out things) as an engineer. I don't like to miss that out because it was a great influence. First of all I was working with engineers and they taught me how to draw, not fancy architectural drawing, but to put down exactly what was going to be built. We were building buildings tremendously fast; they had to be finished in order to make the stuff to put in the bombs. And so the pressure was just unbelievable for three-and-a-half to four years, quite unbelievable. Then we were working in Wrexham in North Wales, in the country, and I had a bicycle, so every day, riding to the office and back, or even looking out of the office window, I could do my natural history. In the office I even had an aquarium tank where I bred dragonflies to the astonishment of all the other engineers. And of course the ordnance factory was enormously spread out and the buildings were all surrounded with mounds of earth to stop the explosions hitting the next building – 800 buildings, each with a mound round it – so I learnt the hard way about slopes and how to use grass on banks, and earth-moving and blade-graders. It was really interesting stuff.

After that, towards the end of the war, all that came to an end and I was in a bit of a fix. I didn't know whether to join the Army (which I didn't want to do because the war was nearly over) – it was the end of '43 or '44. I wrote to Abercrombie whom I hadn't seen for quite a long time and said 'look, I don't know whether you can give me any advice, but what would a man in my position sensibly do?' And he said he was just setting up the Greater London plan, and would I like to join it? I did, in a junior capacity. I did the new town plan for Ongar and I did all the perspectives and I was in charge of the reproduction of the plans. I really got to know Abercrombie, whom I had known of course differently when I was a boy. Now I suddenly met this wonderful man at the height of his career. He was doing many other things at the same time. He was doing Plymouth after first turning it down about four or five times. In the end they came back and offered him the help of the borough engineer and his staff, and he took it on. It was very different from the London plans – small scale, civic design. But I wouldn't like to leave the subject of London without pointing out how many of Abercrombie's principles got into its planning after the war – the Green Belt, the Parks System, the Density System, all sorts of things are pure unadulterated Abercrombie; I think he was a wonderful influence. Abercrombie was fundamentally a classical architect, but he was immensely liberal in his views and catholic in his interests; he talked about Architecture with a capital 'A'.

In my first two years at Liverpool, I had been in the last two years of the Beaux Arts period there. We rendered St George's Hall in Indian ink on Double Elephant Whatman; we drew the Parthenon, we learned all about the classical orders, we did an Italian palace on a rocky headland, we really had our noses ground; and then in the third year we revolted and did nothing but black and white ink drawings and skyscraper blocks. So we had both these things. When I went into practice eventually, after the planning experience, I did find myself a 'closet classicist'. But of course I was also influenced by what might loosely be called 'the modern movement'. It was everywhere, we were swimming in it; we thought we were wonderfully revolutionary characters in the last few years at school. There was Gordon Stephenson and there were the high blocks, and there was Corbusier. We had a dream – not a very sensible one – that buildings should be plain, white, undecorated, beautiful shining things. It was all atmosphere. It took me quite a long time to realise that the principles are always the same, that height and width and the human scale are permanencies in architecture and you can't turn the whole thing upside down.

After the Abercrombie plan, I was retained in the Ministry (Abercrombie's staff had been paid by the Ministry). I was in the technical section of the Ministry of Town and Country Planning under William Holford, with Gordon Stephenson and Tommy Coote. Hugh Casson was there with us – I shared a room with him for a year or two. Then we did Stevenage. Stephenson and I were the two architects who designed Stevenage and Coote and Claxton were its engineers and then I went to Stevenage as deputy chief architect under Clifford Holliday. I was regarded as being too young at 35 to be chief architect. Gordon Stephenson was going to be that, but he suddenly changed his mind and went off to be professor of Civic Design at Liverpool. I'd also thought of going for that Liverpool job – in fact I did apply for it, and I came out second on the list. If Gordon hadn't changed his mind I would have been professor at Liverpool, which seems very strange. I'm really very glad I didn't. But at Stevenage we had 35 workmen and no money to build a new town.

I spent nine months there doing nothing effective at all, and in the summer of '48 I met my dear friend Derek Bridgwater at an architectural conference in Liverpool. We were walking in the garden at Thornton Hough and Derek said 'Peter, why don't you come to London, chuck the Ministry, and be my partner?' He had, I think, one assistant; he'd survived the war by doing things like scheduling railings for preservation, and all sorts of little buildings like air raid shelters. He had one job, a housing job for the GLC [now disbanded] and I joined him. He said 'we won't earn much money but we can start', and there it was. The first year we earned £900 each and the second £1100 and the third £1500 and so on. It was absolute bliss because Derek was one of the most delightful people I have ever known. He was full of energy and life and very interested in everything but he wanted me to do the designing in those early great days.

I was surprised to find what a lot I had learnt from, first of all, the engineers and the war, and secondly the Ministry. The Ministry was a very, very fertile place in those days. Holford and his team were putting the 1947 Bill through Parliament which had come out of the Abercrombie School of Planning. It really was a revolutionary thing. We were changing the whole of planning and landscape in England and we never looked back on that – the idea that the development rights in the land are subject to planning. So Derek Bridgwater and I had this housing job, and he also had another housing job which had been cancelled. The abandoned work fees were quite considerable, about £4000, which kept us going for a bit; then I got a job through some old friends in the Ministry of Education to do a school in Abingdon. This school and the housing job, the Trinity Estate, Deptford, were the first two jobs we did.

Soon after this, Hugh Casson asked if I would like to do the landscape for the Festival of Britain and part of the Live Architecture exhibition, another part of the Festival, down in the East End at Hackney. This is where I found I was a closet classicist. They came to us really for some four- or five-storey flats in Pekin Close. I said that if the flats were four storeys, half the dwellings could be houses but they thought that was rather difficult. The density there wasn't all that high, I think it was about 126 persons per acre, and we did in fact do half the dwellings as flats and half as houses, little linked semi-detached houses in a row and little terraced houses. Those I thought were really quite a success. Houses, of course, got less subsidy than flats, so we had to do them cheaply. The houses cost £1200 each and they were made with sand-lime bricks. I learned then that sand-lime bricks shrink and I never used them again. The point we were trying to make was that modern new housing could be put into an old environment and still reflect the scale and character of the old. The surrounding houses, although shabby and very old, were nicely planned, those little East End Victorian houses of about 1840 were really good little houses. And of course if we'd had any sense and the government had had any sense, they would all have been rehabilitated and renewed with their little old gardens and everything. What we were really doing was to take that scale as our base and say that that kind of house can be done at high densities – we were really doing what Trystan Edwards said could be done.

I remember a story there. When I did my town planning exam – I did it externally because of my research scholarship – they'd

GLC Housing, Gough Grove, Stepney; 3 & 4 storey flats round 90 ft courts.

set a question about density and I had led off with a terrific attack on Trystan Edwards saying how it couldn't possibly be done, you had to have high buildings. When I got to the oral exam, who should have been the oral examiner and who should have set the paper but Trystan Edwards himself; he gave me a very bad time. But we became friends and he used to send his books to me afterwards. We had such an argument over that exam, but of course, quite soon I realised that he was absolutely right.

Hackney was one of our first attempts. After that we remained very interested in low-rise housing at high density. The next site to that old Festival site, Gough Grove, and all the way back to Burdett Road was given to us later on and we did it in our three-to-four-storey style, with flats and little gardens. In the '50s we had done about three high blocks, maybe four, not very high – 11 and 17 storeys. Later we were offered a job by Westminster near Vincent Square and they said they wanted a skyscraper block, but we said we were no longer in that business; we were not going to do any more high blocks. My partner Gabi Epstein had been talking to a housing manager in Hackney and she told him a story about a woman who lived on the seventeenth storey of a block with a daughter of three-and-a-half. She had to keep it secret from her daughter when she was going out for a walk, she said, because the child got so hysterical with delight. What is wrong with high blocks is that they are not connected to the ground, you can't lean out of the windows and call Johnny in to dinner; you are a prisoner. The child was a prisoner in that flat and that's not good for anybody. So we really did have this sort of 'Road to Damascus' experience of saying 'no, we can't do it any more.'

Our few high blocks were not too bad as blocks go, but I regret even these; we were wrong there. This was way back in the '50's. After we had turned down the Westminster block we didn't get a housing job for nearly four years. Then Camden Council came along and asked us to do two high blocks and we said 'No. But we really want this job, please let us do it in four- and five-storey blocks.' And they said it was impossible; but Lacey, I think it was, the housing director, said 'OK, let's have a go'. And we did it. 140 rooms per acre, one-to-one parking, plus 12 artists' studios in four or five storeys and it won the housing medal for the year. Every other scheme in for that medal for that density was 20 or so storeys high. I was really very proud of that; it still looks reasonably decent. Then when we got to the Gough Grove scheme we did even better in three and four storeys instead of four and five. I remember a marvellous experience after Gough Grove was finished and we were showing the housing chairman round. We were on one of the balconies; the balconies were already hung with flowers, flower boxes and baskets everywhere – people, if they like their place, often do that. While we were all standing there on the balcony, an old lady popped out of one of the doors and shouted across to a flat on the other side, 90 feet across the courtyard: 'Liz, come over, I've got the kettle on for a cup of tea.' And you know, this was absolutely a demonstration of what we were after; I remember saying to the housing chairman, 'you can't do that in a high block, you can't look down four floors and call someone up to tea.' Then after that, of course, came the Ronan

Point disaster and everyone started saying that high blocks were unsafe. We would love it if they were but unfortunately they're not. You have to dynamite them, and enlightened councils are doing just that.

In the old days of neighbourhood planning, we thought that people *ought* to have a sense of community. I now think we can't say people *ought* to do anything, but if people live in nice compact housing near to proper shops and schools and nice gardens and everybody is reasonably close to one another, you achieve a human scale and then a sense of community grows up. It's not a thing you can ask for. If people live isolated in high blocks insulated from the ground and from each other, it doesn't happen. A person can die in a high block and six weeks later they know he's dead because the smell comes under the door. That's the kind of thing that is happening. Then community spirit flounders, it doesn't grow. It can't grow in that atmosphere. Urban landscape design helps to humanise. After all, it is the total interlinking of housing and landscape which counts. For example, the blocks at Gough Grove were set in green courtyards, three or four storeys high with an open end to the south, and if possible the blocks going north–south lower than the ones going east–west, so that you trap the sun in the courtyards. Then of course we tried to get as many cars out of the way as possible, and we put them in places where they didn't invade the main spaces. So we suddenly found ourselves with a lot of very fine sheltered bits of landscape. Of course there are problems – where do you put the children's playgrounds so that they don't annoy everybody and so on; but one way and another it's the human scale of the buildings that make the landscape.

The architectural concept which Corbusier put forward, and which had a malign influence, was that the landscape of the high rise would be the visual park-like setting for the high buildings. But that becomes a desert, an unprotected space which nobody is responsible for. Unfortunately it was a view that prevailed horribly. Quite recently, Oscar Newman has been talking about 'defensible space'. I remember Ian McHarg saying I ought to meet him because 'he's talking about just the things you are talking about'. I said 'No, he's talking about the things we've been building for 20 years'. It was amazing how long it took for architects to see it. But the people did. North of Gough Grove there are some of the old high blocks and the housing authority had piles of letters from people living in the high blocks saying 'why can't we go down and live in the lower ones?' The density is the same, you see, this is what is so upsetting. It really can be done, up to about 150 to the acre in four storeys.

The Festival of Britain

The beautiful thing about the Festival of Britain South Bank Exhibition was that we suddenly had a vast pedestrian area with 37 acres and no cars in it, but lots of people. We were forecasting that there might be tens of thousands of people; in fact there were

75 000 people there on the top days. And of course some people were saying it wouldn't work; Sir Albert Richardson, President of the Royal Academy at that time, said it would be a disaster, panic would ensue, people would be trampled to death; of course it wasn't true. What we did was to plan the circulation so that people could move round and find places where they could stop, eat, sit and so on. After planning the circulation, there gradually occurred places which we kept trying to rescue, where there could be real landscape, where nobody would have to walk. One did the circulation plan, then one looked for the interstices 'the space left over in planning' ('sloip' was a term that I coined at the time and which the *Architectural Review* later took on). But this left-over space, if it was planned so that people didn't trample on it, could be very, very elaborate indeed, like the little moat garden for example near the Lion and the Unicorn Pavilion. That moat was a fence to prevent people leaving without paying for their tea. On the other side of the moat of course was a very protected place that nobody could reach, with a boulder-strewn shore, where you could have a very elaborate planting of delicate plants, such as irises. There was a mound beyond the moat planted thickly with shrubs; from outside you saw just the mound and shrubs – the flowers were hidden. This was a principle I have had ever since I began – flowers are made to be looked at at close quarters. In the distance, flowers look like waste paper, so always arrange for flowers to be sheltered, to be come upon in a hollow, or enclosure. Often in the wild you get them in the ditches, in the rivers, in glades; you don't get great displays of flowers in the open unless it's on an enormous scale like the desert in spring. The Festival was full of these little enclaves.

Of course, the planting was a terrible problem, because the Festival opened on May 1st. We had all the plants grown in containers ready to be put out but even then you can't get much of a show by May 1st. It looked a lot nicer the following year. Among the container plants we had *Heracleum mantegazzianum* and *Crambe cordifolia* and others of that kind, real weeds, which made a wonderful display the first year because we had them grown the year before. The Festival taught us a great deal about paving and the kind of fencing which just guides people off grass; not fences but just changes of level and kerbs and things. Just before the Festival design was due to be completed (I think it was actually six weeks before) they cut a million pounds off the budget and as the buildings were nearly finished most of it had to come off the landscape. All the landscape that had been designed as York stone had then to be concrete slabs; what had been concrete slabs became tarmac; what had been tarmac became gravel. That taught me a lesson about the value of the stuff you put on the ground.

Frank Clark also worked on the Festival; I had already met him and was very fond of him. He was in charge of the whole of the Festival landscape and he had at his right hand Maria Parpagliolo Shephard, who was an absolutely wonderful person. What Frank would have done without her, God only knows, as Frank wasn't all that dynamic; but she was. She ordered all the plants and kept everything in line. She was so practical, imaginative, enterprising. I always thought her landscape design was amongst the best I have ever seen. She did a lot of beautiful work for the Italian war cemeteries. She was such a golden creature and I learnt a lot from her. Maria died far too young, very, very sad for English landscape.

It was arranged that Frank was in charge of organising the whole landscape project and designing a small central area with Maria; and Youngman was given the upstream section to design and I was given the downstream section. They were the two sides of Hungerford Bridge. My side had the Festival Hall in it. His was slightly larger than mine and had rather more open areas like the big space outside the Dome of Discovery. There was quite a different flavour in the design of the two sides and there were some differences in the technique. I have always been a fanatic about falls in paving; I don't like puddles. On the other side, I think Youngman's landscape was probably nicer than mine and was more crowded with people which was more difficult; but with his big area , he was faintly optimistic about the paving falls and of course the Festival workmanship was done in such a hurry,

Festival of Britain South Bank Exhibition 1951. The moat garden of the Lion and Unicorn Pavilion.

so he had puddles and I didn't and I used to tease him about it. But the nice thing about the Festival was that it did set all kinds of ideas going, both in buildings and landscape, some of which people laugh at now. I still think it showed that buildings could be interesting to ordinary people in many ways and when it came to the landscape, that really was a new thing. Nobody had done that kind of landscape in England recently, great areas of real public space; the landscape was genuine innovation.

It also became possible after that to show what opportunities you get in landscape without cars. In the office right at this minute, we are rehabilitating housing projects which were done in the 1930s, blocks of flats four or five storeys high whose whole courtyards are covered with black tarmac, mainly for cars; we can rearrange it and put all the landscape back. It's amazing what a difference it makes. It could have been done at any time, but the Festival demonstrated it clearly.

'Modern Gardens'

Contemporary with the Festival work, the Architectural Press wanted a picture book on gardens. They had done *Modern Houses* by F.R.S. Yorke and *Modern Gardens* sounded a rather good idea. So we collected pictures of gardens by people whose work I had known, like Burle Marx and Holger Blom. I thought if we put together a series of pictures of what was being done in the best modern gardens we'd have a very pretty book. Then I took a summer holiday in Aberdovey and spent each morning writing a page of the book so there were twelve pages of introduction. Now those twelve pages were really hard work – I sweated over that to see how much I could put down of what I felt at the time.

I think the most important sentence in it is the first one, where I say that it's very difficult to talk about a 'modern' garden. Modern architecture at that time was architecture made of different materials from what had been used before; concrete, steel and glass had changed the character of modern architecture. I don't think, looking back now, that materials should have been allowed to change it so much, because the *principles* of architecture – the scale, the friendliness and the humanity of it – are still the same. But at least architects had an excuse. The landscape architects, on the other hand, were still doing the same things that Capability Brown did; if you mess about with the topsoil and destroy the environment for plant life, it's all exactly the same as it was in the 18th century. You've now got machines instead of men with spades, but you can still make a mess of the topsoil with machines. I had a very strong sense that modern gardens had to be in the tradition if they were going to be successful. And I think this is the essential thing about landscape architects; they can't get out of the trees, they can't say 'let's see if pigs can fly' like architects can. Architects can say 'let's all live in glass skyscrapers with huge beautiful landscapes in between'. Landscape architects can't have these vague dreams because they are rooted in the earth. This is the background to everything I believe.

I quote Jekyll quite a lot, which doesn't seem to fit in with my hatred of Victorian gardens. I suppose that in that book I did say some very nasty things about them. I remember saying that it is difficult to imagine how fantastic they really were in their heyday, when you had great circles of beds in the middle of lawns with Paulownias – which you cut down every year to get the leaves three feet across, surrounded by cannas and enormous purple cabbages and God knows what. It must have looked very, very grotesque and strange. I still think that a lot of those gardens look much nicer now that their carpet-beddings have disappeared. But Jekyll was out to reform that style of gardening and maintained that it wasn't the fault of the plants that that kind of gardening didn't work. When her visitors expressed surprise that she was planting geraniums on her terrace (pelargoniums), she pointed out that 'bedding plants are only passive agents in their own misuse and that a geranium was a geranium long before it was a bedding plant.' I think that's the key really, that gardening has to be rooted in the real qualities of its materials.

It could be argued that the bedding-out style is an extension of the architectural character of the house. They did, I suppose, use a crude kind of geometric pattern, chopping beds up into funny circles and crescents, but it was't serious architecture. I am quite fond of geometrical gardens, in fact I think that I have now, at the end of my life, arrived at a picture of what I think is the essence of the designed garden; that is, strong architectural lines overlaid by plants, so that the firm lines are all softened and complicated by vegetation. I don't mind how rectangular, or how linear or how geometrical the garden gets; when plants come in, the counterpoint between plants and architecture softens the geometry and the softening can go a long way.

If you look at the big Italian gardens like Villa d'Este, with all those ferns and huge cypresses which come in, these are essential parts of the whole. I believe that in this classical business you can of course *overdo* the architecture in the garden. I think the Italian gardens are absolutely wonderful, but when you get to Versailles or Schönbrunn, the architecture begins to dominate. If you go back to Spain and look at the Moorish gardens, which are totally architectural, totally surrounded by buildings, somehow when it comes to the garden itself, there is a marvellous architectural frame, very severe, and then plants all folding over it contra-puntally. It comes directly from the original Persian gardens; they made these enclosures in the desert and the enclosures were very rectangular, formal, very regularly divided up, and then they had a theme also of the symbolism of the garden with a square and the four parts and a centre – a very geometrical kind of symbolism. Then the water and the plants came in and softened it and brought in movement and life and growth.

I think the English have always been hopelessly half-hearted about classicism – you could not do the Versailles parterre in England; somebody would get tired of it, somebody would give up and let it go, not only the parterres but the avenues, the grandeur. The classicists tried very hard, but in the end the English are not powerful enough, their princes are not rich enough and they don't follow it through. So that the successful classical garden in England is always like Gertrude Jekyll working with Lutyens where you get the architecture and the plants in this wonderful partnership. What I find depressing is the sort of parterre in which all the plants could be – and sometimes are – replaced with coloured marble, gravel or even coal; they would do just as well if they were made of plastic really. They were made to stay like that and be seen from a distance or above. They have little to do with plants, you can't feel about them like Linnaeus felt when he found the harebells growing in the joints of the steps at Uppsala.

I first met Burle Marx quite recently, in the last 15 years, and he told me that my book had got to South America, but I've not had as much talk as I would have liked with him. I find him wonderfully sympathetic because he loves and understands plants. He decided that in Brazil gardens have got to be made of Brazilian plants which were then totally neglected – he had to found his own nursery to grow them. I think one criticism which was levelled against him was that he was really a painter. He is a very good painter, but they said he conceived his gardens as paintings, as things to be hung on the wall and looked at from 90 degrees. There's something in that. He has taken his pattern-making further than I would. For example he has done lawns of reddish, yellowish and greenish grass and separated the grass by little underground steel bands. I don't find this very interesting, but he is a superb plantsman and a great artist.

The gardens I like best of his are the ones like his own garden where the plants really take over. In Brazil, of course, it is easy to get the plants to take over, but I think it can be done here too. I am very sympathetic to the picturesque and the jardin anglais; I think it's so much part of the English landscape. The genius was to realise that 'all nature was a garden'; that a slight adjustment, a little bit of mowing, a little bit of pushing around, a little bit of damming up a stream, could actually create a wonderful landscape – an artificial landscape, but one which could endure. The cows and the sheep would do the mowing and the whole thing would be planned according to what could be managed and maintained. It was an extension of farming, really, and I find that intensely suitable to the landscape. It doesn't have much to do with urban landscape, when the whole landscape is full of buildings, roads and cars and everything else; then you are back with a different kind of scale. Like the garden outside a house, you are back again to your bits of landscape which are 80 and 90 feet wide.

I see a kind of continuous gradation from architecture to the most wild landscape. But England has almost no natural landscape. If you go to America, you are suddenly faced with what they call a wilderness. There isn't any of it in England. I suppose there may be a few acres in Dorset and a few acres in Scotland that haven't been burnt or cut over but on the whole the landscape has been remade. Even Hampstead Heath, which is regarded as a natural landscape, is actually man-made and must be man-maintained. It is now being totally ruined by sycamore trees. Unless somebody does some chopping down on Hampstead Heath, that sort of beautifully developed heathy sand-pit land-scape that it was will disappear. There are probably contradictions in my feelings that architecture and garden can be very happily blended with the idea that nature can come right up to the house. I'm not sure that the whole thing isn't made of contradictions. That's what's so nice about it! I'm not quite sure whether the countryside ought to come up to the door of the house. Brown had to have a ha-ha to stop the cows getting on to the lawn. But most people don't live in country houses; most people live with neighbours, and when you come to the individual neighbourhood, then I think the garden is an extension of the house, an outdoor room. There ought to be a place outside where you can be rather private; in fact these gradations of privacy between house and garden are awfully important.

If there is one thing I've learnt in the last 30 years, it is that we should do a lot more looking backwards, for knowledge and for understanding. If you look backwards you will see what succeeds and what doesn't. You look backwards for the tradition; you find out what are the threads that make it possible. I am even more a traditionalist now than I was, especially in landscape, because I think that when you look at the Japanese gardens, or the Moorish gardens, or the Italian hill gardens, you learn direct lessons which can be used in Hackney or wherever. I don't think it is just a matter of cheering yourself up or getting inspiration; it is finding out what works and what doesn't work. And as I said in my book, the tradition of gardens is still much more alive because of the materials used. Plants haven't changed, soil hasn't changed, drainage hasn't changed, so you learn things directly from the tradition. I think an awful lot of nonsense is talked about the classical or romantic or formal or informal and the argument in the Victorian times between Blomfield and Robinson was largely irrelevant.

Jekyll is the perfect example of the person who really looks hard at nature. I remember Goodhart-Rendel, the architect, telling me once – he was a distant cousin of Jekyll – that he believed that she had made Lutyens into a real architect. He came to her aged 22 and she made him build her a house. She turned his first design down. She didn't want a lot of 'architectonic inutility' but a real house that she could love, of stone and slate and oak and no nails, but wood dowels and things like that, and Lutyens, according to Rendel, took that wonderfully well. Certainly he made her a beautiful house and built nine or ten more houses in the next few years, all masterpieces, in which she was deeply involved. Even when she was 80, he was still writing to her about Delhi; they were real collaborators. What is wrong for me with modern attitudes to the great Renaissance tradition is that people get confused between the boring symmetries of Le Nôtre and Versailles and so on and the excellent site planning and design of the Renaissance gardens of Italy. If you look at an Italian garden like the Villa Gamberaia, you see a marvellous example of site planning – the appreciation of the contours and the hill and how much variety can be packed into a small space. It is not like Versailles, which is ruling a huge landscape by laying down avenues and lines. The Villa Gamberaia is a very architectural garden; but its beautifully detailed adjustment to its site is in the spirit of the Moorish gardens on the hills of Granada.

Jekyll drew her inspiration from nature, of course. She started life as a painter which meant she had an eye, but I think of those passages in her books where she describes nature. In *Wood and Garden* she mentions 'a little wild valley whose planting wholly done by nature I have all my life regarded with the most reverent admiration.' It had holly and thorn and many rugged junipers. She has her own pictures of these junipers, some wrecked by the snow. I always think these dreadful modern gardeners must look at this and think 'what on earth is she talking about – broken-down juniper bushes?' But that passage is really important; it described how this marvellous little dell in the downs which was first grazed by the sheep, then colonised by the junipers, and then battered by the elements had become a numinous place; this is what it's all about. This is your raw material, it's more than inspiration; this is the way the world is made. I find this absolutely enchanting. One of the troubles with old gardens is that you can't be sure what they looked like. Even in Jekyll's gardens, if you look at them now, in these modern photographs, all sorts of little things that she did have been ruined. For example, that long rill in the Deanery Garden which is supposed to be a slit in the lawn, full of irises – a very curious strange thing; in the photos, it has little beds of forget-me-nots and stuff planted down the sides. The steps that go down to it, which should land on the grass, land on a nasty little bed of annuals. Many great gardens are ruined by this sort of thing; gardens are very fragile things.

Education for Landscape Design

Natural history, architecture and history must form the basis of any landscape syllabus. The problem one is stuck with is the way professionalism has developed over the last years. In the 18th century, there were no categories of landscape architect or architect, or anything else. The architect just emerged. What was Capability Brown? He built more houses than gardens. William Kent – was he an architect or a landscape architect? Was Vanbrugh an architect, for he did stage designing half the time? Architecture was just designing the environment.

It became convenient for architects to become professional and specialised and split off from engineers, and to have separate quantity surveyors; then to have landscape architects and planners. But they should all be doing the same thing, instead of each claiming to be the ones who really know. That's fatal, absolutely fatal because nobody knows everything. It may be necessary to have these specialisations (I think it probably is) but the important thing is to get these people together. Holford, at Liverpool, had the idea that the way to train planners was to take geographers, architects and geologists, and all sorts of people and give them two years of joint training which would turn them into men of all trades. It would teach them just enough about the other professions to know how to collaborate with them. I would have all people going in for 'the environmental professions' as I want to call them, do the first year at least, if not the first two years together, and then when they are half-way through their professional education, they could decide whether they wanted to go in the architectural direction, or the planning direction or the landscape direction. But the things that *everybody* has to know, like how the world works – what is the hydrologic cycle, what do plants do and fundamental things like what is human scale, and how do our cities function – those things ought to be common, not put on afterwards, but common to everybody.

In the first two years I would like to teach *all* those people the essence of plant and animal life. I would like them to just know how the world is constructed; I think that is vital. Not only would I like those who are going to be in the environmental professions to know these things, but the public too, and I think some very interesting things are happening here. People like Attenborough and Bellamy are teaching the public more about ecology than some of the landscape architects know; I think this is a good thing. These natural landscapes that people are beginning to make are splendid; they are not being made by landscape architects, but by local boy scouts and volunteers. You see I think you have got to have that knowledge for much more important reasons than just for landscape design. If you live in a country this size, with 60 million people, you've simply got to organise it in a very different way, or you are going to kill the place.

Wallace Decorative Arts Gallery, Williamsburg Va., USA. Garden Court, 1986.

But still I think landscape education is, on the whole, a lot better than architectural education. At many of the architectural schools, the students are brought up in a kind of hothouse atmosphere of architectural design and they get a frightening conviction that architectural design is terribly important stuff; but it really isn't all that important by itself. If you had the whole of the city designed by the best architects and you didn't do anything about the landscape you would still have a disaster.

The Americans have a greater social awareness which is largely being pressed upon them by the social disaster of the cities. We have the same problem here; it's not quite so acute, but it's growing. But what happens is that the sociologists and the people who specialise in planning are saying that architecture is no good, landscape is no good, nothing is any good, you ought to ask *us*. They are committing the same old sin. I think if you build a human scale landscape and if you have a nice aspect and the sun comes into the rooms and if you have a pleasant place for the kids to play, then the social problem will begin to solve itself. The moment you go to a new housing scheme with ordinary working people living in it, you can see whether it's going to work. If it is, the grass is green and the houses are clean, curtains are hung and it's a nice place to be. You go into a tower block of flats and you'll find that not only is it not working and the people are lonely, but it then starts to get really shabby and people shit in the lifts and pee on the staircases and it becomes absolutely intolerable; and in both cases the architect has had quite a lot to do with it. Also of course the social management of the thing may be wrong, but when it works the architecture and the landscape are just elements of good sociology.

Urban parks, on the other hand, are getting better now. In the old days I would have bitten the legs of the parks people; they really were doing badly and there were very few good examples. But it's improved a lot lately and if you look at something like the GLC parks, there is a lot of good stuff going on. I still think that they are very jaundiced about landscape architects and planners, but they may be partly right. I think it's easy, too easy, to criticise the parks people. They had a bad time because they were not training the right kind of gardeners. I believe that one of the things you have to do with a park, being not a garden but splendid open landscape, is to have different standards and skills of maintenance; a lot of parks people were trained to do a different job from the one they are in; they were still being trained to do Victorian bedding and gardens and they were really not happy unless they were clipping and tidying and mowing, and keeping people off the grass. But now there is another whole dimension which is creeping into the parks, a lot of very good landscape, wild stuff and nice hardware.

There is a whole fallacy about the parks which was built in to start with. They were conceived by the Victorians as places where the 'pale mechanic' can take his family for a walk. Places like the northern cities and the London slums were getting so bad that you had to have 'lungs' where respectable people could go and take the air. I think that is a bad concept. We were careful in the London plan to say what you need is a *park system*; it's not parks and then miles and miles of nothing. It's lots and lots of little green spaces which people can use every day.

If you had accessible children's plots, tennis courts, playgrounds and walking places everywhere, you wouldn't then have to travel *en famille* to Victoria Park. You would use it every day, on the way to somewhere else. In the London plan, Abercrombie wanted to thread London through with comparatively small strips and patches and 'spaces left over' as landscape system. Here is a bit which really doesn't need any buildings, let's make a neighbourhood park of it.

In my *Gardens* book for the Design Council (1963), I laid emphasis on the importance of skills and techniques. I think the standard of skill in landscape and indeed in a lot of building nowadays is much better than everybody thinks. The notion that craftsmanship is dead I think is absurd. My new house was built by a 21-year-old foreman and a few other men aged about 25, and they built it in six months and built it very nicely. But, returning to the book, the Design Council had a mental picture of a family which had just moved into a new house and the outside garden was a little square of concrete and clay, and what do they do next? I wanted to do rather more than that by writing about the pleasures of designing your own small garden. This book is directed to amateurs, although a lot of the stuff is very suitable for landscape architects. But people make little ponds themselves and they make them of plastic coloured blue. This little book asks what is a pond — is it a reflection pool? It only reflects if its base is black, so have a black base or have some mud on the bottom. It's everyday amateur technique that I wanted to get at. I didn't include plans because I didn't want to say here is plan A for a family of six, and B for a batchelor and here is plan C; I don't think that helps. What I wanted to talk about was what is a path, how does a terrace work, what are edgings like? And in fact, if you look at the design of the average amateur garden, the principles are exactly the same as if you were talking to a professional landscape architect. I was pleased that some of the landscape schools used my little book for teaching.

The student should learn to be a craftsman in garden construction. I think even architects ought to get on the job and see how the building is built. Frank Lloyd Wright used to say that you ought actually to build, handle bricks, and I wish everybody could do that. An architect ought to get on the site and see what the bricklayer actually does, how rough his hands are. I think it is even more important with landscape. How can you tell someone how to plant a group of shrubs which arrive from the nursery unless you've done it yourself? How can you tell anybody what to do?

Of course, for the landscape architect, site planning is an absolutely basic skill because he has to interpret — he's not going to kneel about and do all that paving himself — he's got to describe it to somebody else, so he's got to learn how to do working drawings for landscape, not just pretty drawings. He has to do perspective drawings to persuade people to buy the stuff and to get people to understand what he's driving at; but the really important thing is to be able to do drawings which, given to a sympathetic contractor, will actually result in what he wants to do. That's not easy.

There's one absolutely fundamental difference between America and England, in both architecture and landscape; there are no quantity surveyors in the USA. This means that your drawings and the specifications have got to show *everything* and this means of course that all drawings must be finished before the job starts. I know there are lots of failures, but the American builder, on the whole, has much more information to start with and the building takes six months instead of a year and a half.

There's another difference; America has the most rumbustious climate, especially on the East Coast. It's a climate like that of Japan, where it's always either too hot or too cold and you get huge storms coming up the coast. Three years ago, in Philadelphia, there was a storm which gave 13½ inches of rain in three days. Can you just imagine that? So therefore you must learn about 'run off'. I don't think English landscape architects even know what 'run off' is until they've seen what an American storm can do. And grass lawns in Philadelphia are terribly difficult to keep through the winter. Lots of people plant a winter lawn and a summer one. So you have a much more ferocious climate and it makes quite a difference to the ways you do things. When you go over to California it's all much easier and Seattle is almost like England.

But in design and work I think there is a great similarity between Britain and the USA. The University of Pennsylvania is a pioneer in the ecological education of landscape architects through McHarg and others and this has now spread to a number of other American schools and of course to England too. In the 1950s that was pioneer stuff, but Ian McHarg is right; it's got to be the basis of the whole thing. Unless you know how nature works, you are not going to be a landscape architect. But then of course you get to the point where so much time has to be spent on that in the landscape course, which is only three years, that you have a heck of a job to get any time for design exercises. My role at Pennsylvania has been largely as a design man and I'm not altogether satisfied with that because though I happen to be an architect and a designer as well, I really believe that the design of landscape can only be done by one who loves and understands nature.

Landscape Planning

In America there's a lot of development being carried out in places where large regional changes are being made, like developing uninhabited islands, valleys or big river systems or curing disasters of various kinds. England has been so done over that people think there is no need to plan it, which is not true, of course, because we've now got to the second round. All this rumpus that's going on between the farmers and the people who want to preserve the hedges and so on and what to do with the Norfolk Broads, that's regional planning, landscape planning. To solve the Norfolk Broads problem you need a group of people who understand why the Broads are like they are. Every ordinary human being, the average sensual man, looking at the landscape, can't avoid thinking that it's always been there. People think that God made the English landscape and it's simply not true: every inch of it is man-made.

I'm pretty worried about the effect of massive large-scale farming on the English landscape. Not so much that it will change the landscape – before the enclosures people were worried that the *enclosures* would spoil the landscape. I don't mind open landscape but there is a big danger that farmers are not doing the right thing – that they are being subsidised to do things which would be better not done. You get people ploughing up moorland because they get a grant for doing it, when it might be more economical nationally to do something else with the moorland, such as using it for recreation or for sheep farming. All over Dartmoor and Exmoor people have been ploughing up moorland and putting the subsidy in the bank and then letting it go back to moorland again which is ridiculous. Freedom is important, but I don't see why everybody *should* do what they like in a little country like this. Freedom is a big thing in America too, and God help us, as long as you can get it *called* freedom in America, you can do anything. Freedom is invoked in order to be able to own a gun and do things that might curtail other people's freedom.

I think some of the things our farmers are embarking on are curtailing other people's freedom, or even perhaps offending against life itself, like battery farming. I'm passionate about that. I don't think that's sensible and I don't believe in the profitability of it or the fact that it is feeding poor people; it's not true. People are now finding they can raise pigs in the fields in little straw shelters. No heating, no elaborate buildings, happy pigs and funnily enough they make more profit. I think a lot of misguided stuff is going on in farming just as it is in landscape and everywhere else. But I think that a really

University of Pennsylvania, Philadelphia, USA. College Hall Green (Blanche Levy Park), redesigned by Peter Shepheard as Dean leading a team of faculty and students. The statue is of Ben Franklin.

stupid thing is to assume, as I once heard a geographer say, that we really don't need the countryside any more; we can have all our cows in underground hangars in the cities and the countryside can be left for recreation. Who on earth does he think maintains the countryside? The farmers are the gardeners of the landscape; they must maintain it, otherwise the countryside will go back to scrub. One person I admired tremendously was Nan Fairbrother, with her wonderful book *New Lives New Landscapes*; that hit this right on the nail. She was way ahead of her time: this was a whole new dimension; and her last two books were seminal works.

I think we should try to produce more regional landscape planners on the American model who could look comprehensively at the problems of the farm and the forest landscape. Of course some of the American planners would be able to act as consultants here, but they would find the conditions very different. Take New Jersey, probably the most highly populated area in America. It has an area of some 1500 square miles which is the pine barrens, an absolutely wonderful unique ecological environment, little pine trees and sand. Now it's beginning to be 'developed' for suburbs, and it's very sad. But there is something much more important than that – all these suburbs are on septic tanks and all the nitrogen is going down through the sand and polluting the aquifer. They now have a water shortage in New York; there is enough water under the pine barrens to supply the whole of the area, yet they are poisoning it with their stupid development. That's the kind of problem. McHarg found the same problem in Minneapolis-St Paul. Here were these twin cities and Ian did a regional plan to suggest where their suburbs should grow. He found just the same thing there, that the amount of nitrates in the water was already enough to produce so many blue babies per thousand. But the interesting point was that a town like that is deciding where its suburbs should extend to and they are extending into *forest*; there is a great deal of open land there. Now England is one fortieth of the size of the USA, we have no wild forest, all the soil is used up and there is very little space. The problem is not deciding what to do with vacant pieces of land; it's deciding how to rearrange the existing land – to create a new landscape pattern on an existing landscape.

Then, of course, if a piece of land has already been used for hundreds of years, you get all sorts of vested interests like the farmers, and fishermen, and everyone else, which are all part of this problem. I think pollution is being relatively well dealt with in England in some ways; the cleaning up of the Thames for instance is a fantastic success, and if you can do that with the Thames then there's no problem, relatively speaking, about Merseyside or Middlesbrough. Similar things are happening to some extent in America. They've got shad going up the Delaware again. I think this kind of thing is a landscape responsibility.

One lesson we could learn from America is how much can be done by public opinion. America's planning laws are weak compared to ours which, however weakened by recent government amendments, still give strong powers to regulate land use . But in America public participation is strong, and though a somewhat negative force – better at preventing things than promoting them – it can be mobilised swiftly to protect threatened landscapes. It may yet preserve what remains of the New Jersey pine barrens.

In Britain, there is much to be done, and it is *urgent*. Let me end with the wise saying of F. Fraser Darling which Nan Fairbrother quoted on the flyleaf of her book: 'We can be of little service to our fellows until we become disillusioned without being embittered.'

Brian Hackett

Brian Hackett qualified as architect, planner and landscape architect and has an MA degree from the University of Durham. The major part of his career has been concerned with landscape education, in particular as senior lecturer, reader and ultimately professor of Landscape Architecture at the University of Newcastle-upon-Tyne. He is both fellow and past president of the Landscape Institute (1967 to 69) and one of the first members (and chairman) of its education committee. He was awarded the European Prize for Nature Conservation and Landscape Development in 1975.

Early Life

I was born in Bideford in 1911. Both of my parents had artistic backgrounds which may well have had some influence on my subsequent work as a landscape architect.

On my father's side was the firm of Thomas William Camm, who were distinguished stained glass artists right through the 19th century and, in fact, until just after the 1939/45 war. The very last window that they made was a wartime memorial window in St Mary's, Warwick. That was the last of the line and the firm has completely died out, unfortunately, although it was suggested that I ought to go into the firm when I left school. That was in the 1929/30 economic slump; as a result it was thought that that was not perhaps a very wise thing to do and was one of the reasons why I was steered towards building architecture. I ought to mention that my father was a professional musician.

The artistic background comes through on my mother's side too, because her mother was very interested in art and new artists in the Birmingham area, and she was a collector of antique furniture and paintings. My mother influenced my reading – she was very keen on reading – and read Dickens and Walter Scott to us as children. This is something which seems to be quite lost these days – parents actually reading every evening for about half an hour, going right through novels. My grandfather on my mother's side, by contrast, was managing director of what was then, I think the Birmingham and Midland Railway Carriage Company, which is now Metro Cammell Laird. So perhaps I had an advantageous background with art on one side and technology on the other.

As a small boy I was brought up close to the countryside and then subsequently we moved and I went to school at Burton-on-Trent. This was a smallish town and we frequently made picnics and excursions into the countryside. In those days one could cycle in the countryside in reasonable peace and quietness and as a boy, I enjoyed this. We were always keen on going for holidays to wilder places too, for example, Anglesey. We used to go to Rhosneigr, a very small seaside place, and we would walk ten or so miles a day as a family, all the way round the South Stack lighthouse, places like that; so that as a family we were very keen on getting out and exploring the countryside (as opposed to holidays in sophisticated towns like Brighton or Llandudno); and I think this experience certainly had an influence on me.

When I left school, which was towards the end of the 1920s, no one there had ever heard of a landscape architect. The school I attended – a very good grammar school providing rather a fundamental education – was one of those very old Henry VIIIth foundation schools, but as for the school being able to give one any advice on how to follow a career, other than a purely academic one, it was absolutely hopeless: careers advisers hadn't yet been invented. As I was good at art, my father managed to arrange for me to stay on in the sixth form and to be excused homework so that I could attend the local School of Art in the evenings. There was a gifted architect who taught some architecture at this School of Art (simply because of the economic situation) and he subsequently became a teacher at the Architectural Association in London – a very good architect by the name of J.M. Clarke. He certainly had an influence upon me. Also, whilst I was still at school, every week I used to go out into the countryside and sketch an old church or mansion, research into its history, and write a popular article which was published in the weekly newspaper in Burton-on-Trent; I was paid the princely sum of ten shillings for each one.

At that stage of my life I was mainly interested in architecture and painting. I used to copy some of the well known Italian paintings from illustrations in books I borrowed from the local library. I knew little about landscape and hadn't even heard of landscape design as such, but nevertheless the fact that I was more interested in buildings in the countryside rather than in towns, may have been indicative of things to come.

My only practical interest in gardening as a child was when we moved into another house in Burton-on-Trent, when I was about to leave school. Previous to that, our back garden was used mostly by my brother and myself to play cricket, but when we went to the new house, there was a much better garden and together with my mother, I began to cultivate some vegetables and flowers. So we did actually begin to do some practical gardening during my last year at school.

My main memories of the town itself at that time are that there were a large number of independent breweries linked by railway lines crossing the roads. It was a great town for railway crossings and there were mostly late 19th century industrial buildings – rather good ones, in fact, which today architects in London and other cities are remodelling around the Docks. There was not very much dereliction in that particular town, but there was I think a good atmosphere of green space. For example, the River Trent ran through it and the town was divided by the valley of the Trent with recreation grounds and open land. Then, of course, all these brewery companies had their sports grounds which were almost like a green belt round the town, so that I was brought up in a town where the evidence of greenery was fairly strong. The only contact with industrial cities was on occasional trips to Birmingham to have my eyes tested or to visit my relations, but I didn't really come into contact with what one might call industrial dereliction at that time.

Professional Education and Training

I left school when I was about 18. The family were still questioning whether I should go into the stained-glass firm or whether I should go into architecture, because the stained-glass relatives were my father's only advisers, I suppose. Neither was my school able to help very much; it had no idea whether there were any schools of architecture or how to become an architect. The most familiar way at the time seemed to be, at least in a small town, that you became an articled pupil to a firm, but fortunately I was spared that and went to the local art school for a year instead. Then we moved to Birmingham and I was able to attend the Birmingham School of Architecture and work in an office. (Even if one had known anything about landscape design at the time, there were no courses in the country until the Reading course started in the mid-1930s.) I still had not actually made up my mind what I was going to do but the stained-glass relatives thought that owing to the slump, they could really see no future in stained glass. Architecture seemed a firmer basis for a career so I was steered into that, and having done this job of sketching buildings and writing articles whilst still at school, I was rather interested in the prospect.

I look back on that particular part of my education with some pleasure. First of all, it was the only possibility at the time, but in some ways I was obviously lucky in having a bit of a hybrid approach to it, compared with a young man today, who goes to school, does his 'A' levels, goes straight to a school of architecture or landscape and immediately comes under one particular influence. I think perhaps I didn't have such a good factual basis to the design discipline. Also, of course, one had to do more paddling of one's own canoe in those days, although it wasn't a bad thing, even if it took longer to get there. For example, if you go to a school of architecture today, your teachers are top-level architects from the beginning; you get a man who is a specialist in structural mechanics teaching you that part, and another who specialises in building materials and construction, and so on. But I had to study structural mechanics by myself, learning the hard way. There were very few specialists in those days and one had to do a lot more private study and self-teaching.

On the other hand, the design training was very different. First of all, you had to draw a great deal from plaster casts of architectural details. Secondly, you did a certain amount of life drawing and a lot more measured drawings of historical buildings. Design subjects tended to be on the lines of designing a Georgian house, and you were expected to use the historical styles. Whilst I am sure that is frowned upon today, I feel that it is a very good discipline to learn how to do things correctly from the beginning.

The essential skills I think that the art school gave me were the ability to sketch and paint, which I still keep up – I do a lot of watercolour drawings on holidays, etc. It also taught me that there was more in design than assembling rooms and windows and things like that; one also had to look at the actual appearance of what one was designing. It taught me the techniques of drawing and by concentrating (as they made you) on classical orders, on Gothic architecture and so on, you were actually working within good accepted standards of design, as opposed to the rather free-for-all thing these days, where there are few disciplines to contain you.

I have already mentioned the architect J.M. Clarke who subsequently went to the Architectural Association. There was also a teacher who had been head of a school of art in India and must have been in what was then the colonial service, probably retired, who came in middle age to work at the School of Art. He brought this new flavour – he'd got this Indian background – and I think he opened up our eyes to something more in design than the classical and Gothic traditions here. And then at the Birmingham School of Architecture, there was G. Drysdale, an architect trained at the Beaux Arts in Paris; also J.B. Surman a local-trained Birmingham architect who was very good on neo-Georgian buildings. They all had something to contribute.

During the 1930s, I began to feel that building architecture by itself was not really the 'be-all' shall we say of any development. Certainly, in one or two jobs in the office where I worked in Birmingham, we did get opportunities to design gardens and those were given to me, so I had some small opportunity to try and design a garden, although I knew very little about it at the time. It was during this period that I began to hear about planning. Planning at that time was really little more than housing estate development, which seemed extraordinarily narrow to me. I was attracted by the news of a school of planning for national development (subsequently the School of Planning for Regional Planning and Regional Reconstruction) which E.A.A. Rowse started in association with the Architectural Association in London, and was a part-time evening school. Exactly how I heard about it I cannot remember but I discovered that Rowse's approach was completely different from anything else that had gone before and it was far removed from the Liverpool School of Civic Design and the planning course at University College, London. Its scope seemed much wider than merely civic design and town layout, so I decided that I ought to try to get a job in London in order to attend this school. That was in 1937 and I didn't start immediately, as I had to find my feet again in London. I suppose I missed the first week of the course but I got myself work as an architect.

Rowse was a real character! He taught the history of planning the wrong way round, by starting at the present day and going back, instead of starting with Adam and Eve and going on to the present day. Also one came under the influence of geographers, geologists, people who deal with sewerage and soils, all kinds of specialists who came in and gave one or two lectures. Sir Raymond Unwin, who was very involved with what we would call new town development, was also one of my lecturers. He was rather a quiet unassuming chap, rather short as I remember, with a fair amount of white hair and a broad face, and he lectured in a conversational style. He seemed very much an academic and came from a time when designers tended to be real characters, people like Lutyens, Blomfield and Sir Herbert Baker, with very strong personalities so that the client didn't always get his own way with them. I do not think they would have fitted into the modern technological age, where most of the architects have to be good businessmen, and I cannot help feeling that Unwin would have been a bit unhappy in practice today. Nevertheless, I would describe him as a progressive. The fact that he was prepared to give these special lectures in what we might call 'Rowse's outfit', which was a bit revolutionary at that time and would certainly have been frowned upon by a lot of people, I think suggests that he saw planning as much more than straight lines on paper for streets, that it included the total environment. I think that Unwin's book *Town Planning in Practice* showed that he looked at the whole rather than the individual parts. Both Unwin and Rowse had a great sensitivity

The landscape at Rowntree's factory at Newcastle upon Tyne.

for landscape. Rowse, although an architect, had a vision of landscape that took in rural landscape, the effect of agricultural development, the effect of industry in towns, and so on. Detailed landscape design was not his field at all but he gave one a broad vision of planning, making changes to the whole environment.

It was about this time that I was first introduced to the idea of new towns. One of my fellow students called Jeffryes[1] selected a new town as his major scheme at the end of the course, as opposed to a detailed housing layout. Also through the School of Planning, I heard about Mumford and *The Culture of Cities* which was a very new book then and was to become a planner's bible. And, of course, Jacqueline Tyrrwhit was a student with me. You were lucky to get a word in edgeways during or after a lecture by someone like Unwin because Jacqueline was on her feet straight away. She had a tremendously strong personality and was very astute. I don't think one could ever say that she had a great design background but she certainly had the broad vision and a good aesthetic appreciation, as well as a strong social consciousness. She was, I suppose, the sort of person who 30 years later might have been organising CND. She was a leader and I think that has always been her great forte – an ability to get things going. I had also heard of Thomas Mawson[2] of course – I later met one of the Mawsons, although whether it was one of the brothers or one of the sons, I can't say. This was in my early Institute of Landscape Architects (ILA) days. The other interesting thing – and this is rather jumping ahead – is that when I went up to the University of Durham in 1947 to start the landscape course there, I think I am right in saying that there were only two landscape architects north of London: one was Mawson's son in Preston and the other was myself in Newcastle. I quote this to people and tell them that there is now a North East Chapter of the Institute alone with about 60 members – a tremendous difference. One of the snags with an evening course is that you don't get to know people very well, but I do remember Peter Youngman of course, who was also at the School of Planning.

The first task we were given where we actually produced something was a planning development study of Bloomsbury and I believe this was to have been followed by a rural study but war broke out. As a result, I was only there for one year instead of two and everything came to a halt. It was Jacqueline Tyrrwhit who got the course going again by developing a correspondence course for people in the forces and then later, a three-month high-pressure course on which I taught immediately after the war.

The War Years and After

When the war started, I was busy with bomb damage and air raid shelters and then volunteered for the RAF and, to my surprise, having opted for no particular branch, was told when I went up for interview that I was selected for armaments. I was told that there was a problem in that anyone who knew anything about armaments was either making them or already in the forces.

Therefore, what they had to find were people who could cope with, and these were their words, what amounts to a university course in six months.

So, within three or four weeks, I was square-bashing and in another four weeks I was shoved over to the Isle of Man for one week, and after that to No.1 Air Armament School at Manby in Lincolnshire for six months, studying guns and turrets and bombs and bomb disposal and bomb sights, flying and all the necessary theory. Then, of course, as the war began to progress, I remembered that I was only half-way through my planning course and I could see that planning was going to be much more than civic design or housing layout. At first, I thought that when the war was over I would go back into a planning course and spend another year or two on that. On the other hand, I had already been a fully qualified architect for six to eight years and obviously wanted to get back into some earning capacity as soon as possible. So I decided that the best thing to do was to study privately for the final examination of the Town Planning Institute, which I took in uniform and passed.

About this time, I somehow discovered that there was such a thing as an Institute of Landscape Architects, which was then very small. No one seemed to know anything about it, so I made enquiries and eventually got in touch with Sir Geoffrey Jellicoe's secretary, Mrs Browne, who seemed to be the kingpin, and was invited to become a member. I thought this was all very well but I had better show some qualifications to back up my application. I was able to produce a couple of garden designs I had done, together with a short work on landscape in connection with roads which, looking back on it now, was extremely primitive, but was done while I was in the Air Force. I was accepted.

I was demobilised very quickly because there was no use for armament people when the war was over, and was immediately asked via Jacqueline Tyrrwhit, who had kept in touch during the war, to come and teach at the School of Planning on their three-month, high-pressure courses. I did this for a year or year and a half and had students who have become quite distinguished people, many of them about my age or slightly older; here was I, having to teach them and take them out to places like St Albans and sewerage works and so forth, and also work with them on their major design pieces, which they did in the studio. Jacqueline Tyrwhitt and myself were the mainstay in terms of full-time teachers but Peter Youngman came in occasionally, Sir George Peplar, chief planning officer of the Ministry, was the external examiner, and the other teachers were specialists brought in to give lectures in geology, soils and other relevant subjects.

Another influence upon me was the books of Tommy Sharp, which I bought whilst I was in the Air Force and getting ready to take my examinations. His influence was very strong on landscape and that, I think, was another reason why landscape was later so successful in Newcastle. Of course, it was a time when we all thought that planners were really going to take the lead and all the others, the industrialists and the architects, the surveyors and engineers, were going to work under them. It never really worked out like that but the change in planning control and planning development in this country, from what I remember from the '20s and '30s, has been phenomenal. On the other hand, there wasn't this tremendous pace of development then and whilst a lot of our hopes have perhaps not been realised, particularly in the landscape field, a tremendous amount more has been achieved than one could have thought possible.

To give an example of this, I was very impressed recently at one of the meetings at the Social Science Research Council of a small committee to look into the future of grants for landscape students. A professor of geography at London University put forward a case for more help for landscape education. He agreed with me that in many ways it was more important to support landscape than planning in terms of grants because, in his view, over the last 30 years, the thing which strikes you most is the landscape development throughout the UK and the change brought about by landscape architects. You may notice individual buildings, many of them in fact not very pleasant to look at, but the landscape, with the number of trees that have been planted, the amount of greenery and the way the environment has changed as a result of landscape architecture is tremendous and this provides an almost incontrovertible argument for landscape courses. The other area where considerable progress has been made is in the cleaning up of derelict areas.

ILA and Landscape Education 1947–50

I joined the Institute in about 1944/45, at the end of my time in the Forces, and I remember going to what I suppose would have been an annual meeting of the Institute, which must have been the summer of 1946 in Cheyne Walk, Chelsea. That was my first direct contact with such members of the Institute as there were in those days. There could not have been more than about 15 or 16 people at that meeting. Neither can I remember whether it was at that meeting that they put me on the Council, but Council meetings only took place once every three months and involved all the people who were active (about ten or a dozen in number). I can remember Sir Geoffrey Jellicoe, of course, Mrs Browne – his secretary – who did so much for the Institute, and I am certain one of the Mawsons was there. I also remember Milner White, Peter Youngman, Dame Sylvia Crowe, Brenda Colvin, Lady Allen of Hurtwood, Sheila Haywood – who worked in Jellicoe's office for a time – and, of course, Richard Sudell. There was also a man called Gilbert Jenkins, who I don't think practised much landscape but seemed very keen on coming to Council meetings and giving wise advice. Thomas Sharp was also at some of those meetings and subsequently became president of the Institute. There were no committees at that time; all the business was done at Council but it was most inspiring working with those few dedicated people. The Landscape Institute was considered by other professions to be the most vocal per member of any Institute in the country, meaning of course, that we made far more noise even than the Royal Institute of British Architects (RIBA), the Town Planning Institute (TPI) or the Civil Engineers. Yet whereas they had thousands of members, there were no more than about a dozen of us.

The main concern was really education. Very quickly we realised that unless we could establish a sound educational basis for landscape, we really hadn't got much hope of building up the profession. One could not go on indefinitely just finding people who were interested and influential and getting them to back an Institute. Most of us were self-taught as regards landscape although Dame Sylvia Crowe and Brenda Colvin had horticultural backgrounds, but even they had to learn design by working with someone who could design. So education came very prominently to the fore and in order to get things going, we set up a separate education committee. The first real progress we made was when Sir Geoffrey Jellicoe managed to get the cement marketing people (and I think ICI) to put up some money annually for ten years to get landscape education going. I think this amounted to the princely sum of £1200 a year, and there was a certain amount of discussion as to where this should be allocated.

While all this was going on, I was invited by the University of Durham at King's College Newcastle to join the new undergraduate planning course which had just been started, largely, I suppose, because of my experience at the School of Planning. I was appointed as a planning lecturer and was asked to run two landscape lecture courses for planners, as well as planning lectures, one on the history of landscape and another on landscape design, as applied to town and country planning. Very soon, Professor Allen (professor of planning), knowing of my interest in landscape and of my connection with the Institute, and having heard from me that the Institute had been given this money and was obviously looking round for a worthy recipient, said, 'can't we start something going at Newcastle?' It seemed appropriate, since Thomas Sharp taught planning on a part-time basis in the School of Architecture at Newcastle before the war and one or two of his books showed a very strong landscape interest; also Capability Brown was born in the area. Other advantages were the broad scale of the Northumberland landscape and the new Kielder Forest. So we approached the Institute and Professor Allen and I went to London for a meeting at Jellicoe's office. The professor of Fine Art from Reading University was also present. Reading had started a landscape course in the 1930s which, as far as I know, had to close down during the war and they were obviously interested in starting up again. However, the Institute expressed some concern over the way that landscape was divided between the School of Fine Art and the School of Horticulture at Reading, which could have been a problem. Finally, the Institute decided to give half of the money to London University and half to what was then Durham University at Newcastle, which amounted to £600 per year. This was quite gratifying, since nearly all the members of the Institute were Londoners, apart from myself, and they therefore thought that London was the obvious place to set up a course.

In the meantime, I had been changed from a lecturer in planning to a lecturer in landscape and was made one of the first 'senior lecturers'. Nevertheless, the course still hadn't been started and the Institute, not surprisingly, wrote to see what was happening. As a result, Professor Allen and I went to see Lord Eustace Percy [3], who was then Rector of King's College, University of Durham, and in charge of the Newcastle end of the University, to discuss the question of the Institute's having given us £600. We all realised that with this small amount of money, the most we could do was to run a one-year postgraduate course, the kind of course they had already been doing with planning for some years. Lord Percy was generally in favour of starting the course but was concerned as to the possibility of our graduates obtaining jobs. I had to admit that at the time there were no jobs going, even in London, but he thought that there was some hope for the future. I think it is very significant that he did foresee that landscape was something that was going to come. He came to all of the faculty meetings at which the new course was discussed and much was due to his enthusiasm and the fact that he said 'Well, let's do it and have faith in it'. And, of course, we did.

I still attended ILA Council meetings regularly and was made the first chairman of the education committee, which then had the job of setting up the Institute's own examinations. Meanwhile, London University, again after some pressure, set up an evening course in landscape architecture. They were very fortunate in getting Peter Youngman to run it but I think the Institute was a little disappointed not to have a full-time London course. Reading eventually started again with Frank Clark [4] but soon, to my mind, made the very serious mistake of closing that course down. In retrospect, it was an absolutely stupid thing to do.

External Influences

In the late '40s two significant things happened. Firstly, in 1947, I put in for a staff research grant at Newcastle, to spend a couple of months in Sweden studying their landscape work, because I had found out by that time that Sweden was about the only country in Europe which had actually been doing landscape since the 1940s. Secondly, in 1949, the first Fulbright travel grants to America were instituted. There were two kinds of grants: one was for people to study in America, and the other was to enable senior university staff to spend a short time in the States. Realising that America had established landscape education for a number of years, I thought that I should take a look at what had been achieved. I was lucky enough to be awarded one of the first five senior Fulbright grants, so I went to the States, where I was attached to Cornell University in the summer and then went to Iowa University and Illinois University. I spent a week or two in each and found out all I could about how Americans were teaching landscape. As a result of my travels to Sweden and America, I managed to build up a reasonably good background for starting the course at Newcastle. It is not without interest that in 1984, I was asked to join a small group to assess the landscape course in Sweden.

The first three students at Newcastle were Marian Paynter, who subsequently went to Heriot-Watt University in Edinburgh, Brian Blayney, who was, I think, probably the first landscape architect to be employed on landscape reclamation, and Lewis Clarke. I persuaded the latter to try for a Henry Fellowship to visit the States and, rather to our surprise, bearing in mind that this fellowship was open to students from all universities in all subjects, and landscape architecture was virtually unknown academically, he was given one. He went to Harvard University and subsequently taught at the University of North Carolina and had a very strong influence in America. I think it was from those early days with Lewis Clarke that the idea of the ecological approach which we propagated in Newcastle took root in the USA. Now, of course, the Americans have taken this up very willingly. Incidentally, the first time I heard about ecology was via Sir Geoffrey Jellicoe during the war. And then in order to explore this very quickly, I read Tansley's *The British Islands and their Vegetation* which I realised was the basis of his ecological thinking, and I found that a very valuable background. I then began to do research on how ecology could be applied to landscape design.

In Europe, J.R. Benthem and others found that the International Union for Conservation of Nature and Natural Resources (IUCN) seemed with its Unesco influences to be the best medium for spreading interest in landscape planning. Benthem, I think, started off originally as a school master, became involved in what is the equivalent of the Forestry Commission in Holland and eventually ended up as their chief landscape architect. He is another man like myself who never had any training as such but was involved in rural landscape right from the beginning and was also a keen naturalist, an expert on birds and bird watching, so that the ecological approach came naturally. IUCN was divided into the ecological commission, a legal commission, one related to wildlife and so forth; they set up this small sub-committee on landscape planning and asked me to join it. The first meeting I remember of any importance was the one held in Edinburgh in 1953, to which I contributed a paper. I was very much involved until they finally appointed a full-time secretariat and the whole thing became less amateur and was much more influential.

I should like in this context to mention two American examples of landscape planning, the first large scale and the second small scale. Travelling through America by train to the TVA[5] region in 1949, I noticed that the rivers were very muddy, almost like soup, and immediately I got into the TVA area of influence, the waters were crystal clear in the streams and in the lakes. This struck me very forcibly. Obviously, the muddy rivers were due to the erosion of soil taking place, presumably due to forests being cut down and no proper provision being made for preventing erosion. The small scale example came to my attention when visiting some of the agricultural landscape in the TVA area and we were talking to a small farmer. The way he talked to me showed that he had ecological ideas at the back of his mind: 'Well, look up there', he said 'look at that grass stretch that I put in, in order that the run-off of water can run down through the grass. That forms a very stable channel, otherwise the water will simply wash my crops and my seeds out. I just slightly graded the land and made this grass drainage channel, which is fairly stable unless you get a colossal storm.' That was just an example, and there were others, of the way he planned his planting and so on. This all came from him without my questioning him and showed that the TVA's influence extended right down to the farmer. I was very impressed with that and it really convinced me that the ecological approach could work in what you could call a man-made landscape.

Development of Landscape Planning

However, landscape planning has not yet developed as much in the last 20 years as we had hoped as a professional activity and there aren't many people who can claim that they have produced many large scale landscape plans. I believe that one of the main reasons for this is that the UK is a small country which has been highly developed over the last four to five hundred years. The small field pattern which was developed with hedgerows around and the small woodlands that various landowners created, produced an ecological landscape. If you tried to design a landscape where you wanted to produce food and timber that didn't conflict with nature, it would be hard to think of anything better. The result of this is that landowners having worked so satisfactorily in the past, an approach to either the forestry or the farming people brings the question, 'Why do you need landscape planning?' It is only recently with the introduction of agricultural machinery and the vast removal of hedgerows that people are more conscious of the need for landscape plans in the countryside.

I remember travelling down to London years ago when there had been a very early dry spring and a high wind developed so that over the low-lying countryside around the Peterborough area there was a brown pall of what I thought at first was smoke, extending all the way from right to left, which it transpired was the result of soil erosion. The crops had not developed in such a way as to hold the soil together, and that certainly was one of the things that really convinced me that the demolition of our hedgerow pattern accounts for the loss, I suppose, of hundreds of tons of soil each year, without people realising it. So I think the fact that our landscape has been so successful from an ecological point of view for such a long time is a reason why those whose predecessors made it don't take kindly to the fact that, with the world changing so fast, the landscape is also going to have to change and that what we really need is landscape planning to hold it together.

One of the things that should have been done is to provide regional landscape planning for the worn-out industrial areas in this country. There has been a tendency I think for each derelict coal-field or coal-mine to be treated independently and just to restore it, perhaps give it back to the farmer next door (who is very glad to have an extra bit of land), but no-one really looked at all the sites, which are very extensive and are dotted all over the coalfield areas, and the possibility for making sure that the way they were reclaimed fitted into some wider regional landscape plan. I suppose the main reason for giving grants for landscape reclamation was just to tidy the place up. That was the original idea, but the idea of bringing back more of the natural landscape would have fitted in very well with the concept of regional landscape planning.

Landscape planning does, of course, cut across the work of other professions and agencies. For example, in the 1930s the architects were against an Institute of Landscape Architects. But once landscape architects had reached out on large projects and were doing motorways and projects of that size, the architects realised that this was not their cup of tea and were only too glad to bring in landscape architects to work with them. So I don't think that they have been an obstacle to landscape planning. The Forestry Commission has gone a long way to improving the layout of their afforestation works, largely due to the influence of Dame Sylvia Crowe, but has moved up to Scotland, and that is where further development is going to take place. I would have thought that when one is dealing with thousands of hectares of forestry land to be developed, one now needs a national landscape plan for

Detail of the landscape at the Crematorium, Dipton Fell, Co. Durham, in association with B. Robson.

Scotland covering all land uses to carry this out. In fact, this was realised by some people in Scotland a long time ago because there was a National Landscape Plan Conference held near Glasgow in 1963, which I attended. The idea of this conference was to advocate 'the national landscape plan' because of these vast untouched areas of Scotland which were wide open for a developer to move in and now look what's happened! Look at the effect the North Sea oil industry has had. That ought to have been part of a national landscape plan, so I do think that there is still a need for one. It is probably too late now for many parts of England but certainly Scotland, I would have thought, ought to be planned at this level. Neither do I think that the Countryside Commission has furthered the cause of landscape planning as much as it could have done. It was always a matter of regret that it took them some time to employ landscape architects on their staff. I think, to begin with, they were rather devoted to landscape recreation only; then they began to take an interest in the agricultural side but now I think they are developing a landscape planning approach, which is good.

As to where landscape planning should go now, it is difficult perhaps to think of landscape planning for the inner city. I think the landscape architect should be in partnership with the planners and the engineers but I do not know that it is valid to think actually of a landscape plan for an inner city. However, the urban fringe, which is after all a part of the countryside and is the place where the transition between the very man-made landscape of the city and the rural landscape takes place is a very different matter. In my view that is where a landscape plan really needs to start.

Landscape Design and Nature

I am a great believer in modern society developing a much closer relationship with the natural landscape. There was I believe, somewhere in Switzerland, an architect or landscape architect who tried to develop a housing area which had a much closer connection with the natural landscape than was usual. In Holland too they have tried to bring a wilder, natural landscape to housing areas. I can't help thinking that some of the social problems we get in cities are perhaps partly due to the fact that people are not brought up close to the landscape. I was brought up close to the landscape and I think it was a healthy influence. For example, we used to go and do a bit of camping in a field near the home of a friend on the outskirts of the town. There was farmland next door to his back garden and we used to erect a tent and did actually sleep there once or twice. We would go out and cook our meals and play cricket in that field. These were healthy exercises compared with the modern young person in the centre of the city. He may have an adventure playground if he is lucky, but that is not the same as being able to move freely in a large area of open country and being able to put up a tent and start his own camp fire and do some fishing in the stream.

I do believe that ecology has a moral value and that if man

develops an affinity with nature it does remind him that man isn't completely dominant; he has got to work with nature and that suggests a bit of humility. I don't think that humility is a bad thing. I think the urban fringe is, for many people, the nearest one can get to nature for the time being and this needs developing much more as a landscape in which young and old people can get out, not just to play golf and participate in the more disciplined types of recreation. If people can get out into the green landscape and move much more freely, as in fact the wild things do, learning to respect and enjoy their natural surroundings, as we did ten or twenty thousand years ago – I feel that this would be a good thing.

In the eighteenth century Wordsworth, for example, certainly did a lot to 'popularise' (if that is the right word) the Lake District and the idea of countryside; and of course some of the English watercolour painters began to paint the Lake District and other wild landscapes – Turner for example. I can't help feeling that if one is able to appreciate beautiful things, then one's own personality is improved thereby. For example, it is difficult to see how some of the more criminal elements in our society could appreciate the countryside. It is very difficult to know how to put this, but I do feel that if one is able to go to the countryside and know why it is beautiful and to look at it and consciously to enjoy that experience, this does help one psychologically.

Some years ago (about 1967), the Professor of Psychological Medicine at Newcastle and myself tried hard to get a research grant from the Nuffield Hospital Foundation to do research into the landscape of mental hospitals. We believed that some mentally disturbed people may feel much happier in what you might call a wide open landscape – would respond to a sense of freedom. Others may only feel happy in something which is more of a reflection of the back garden in which they live, in other words, they only feel happy in a very small scale landscape that is enclosed and would feel uncomfortable if the doors were thrown wide open. Unfortunately, although the director of the Nuffield Foundation showed an interest in our ideas, we didn't get the grant. It was sad because I think people are probably beginning to realise more and more that one can achieve happiness through landscape. One can even achieve physical health through landscape and I feel that more research needs to be done in this fields too. After all, when a man did live closer to nature 10 000 years ago, I rather doubt whether there were any mental or psychological problems then. Now the experts tell us that a lot of our present psychological problems are due to the particular high pressure of life which is connected with cities. You know, one wonders how many farmers develop psychological problems compared with those people living in cities! I don't know whether anyone has done any research on this but they ought to. This would seem to be a field that is well worth exploring because, after all, landscape is the world we live in and psychologists talk about the environment having an influence on people. Therefore we ought to examine whether the environment needs changing, or people need moving into different kinds of landscape in order to gain the most benefit psychologically.

Books

My first book was largely the result of research and was called *Man, Society and Environment* (1950) and that was, I should think, a very early use of the word 'environment'. Within the last 20 to 25 years, it has become one of the most common words in our language. I was looking at something wider than just physical planning and the book stemmed from my experience at the old School of Planning, where we did try to bring together everything in the environment, not only towns themselves, but also the countryside, agriculture, development of canals and so forth. So that did encapsulate to a certain extent my idea that environment was something more than little bits and pieces. Then I realised that little had been written about landscape design, apart from Brenda Colvin's book and those of Tunnard (1930) and Thomas Sharp (1930s and 1940s). So I did research in the university and tried to find techniques which could be used in landscape planning design theories, principles, and I ended up by having written over 100 papers, all of which have been published in various countries. Then, of course, having got involved in this landscape planning movement, as mentioned earlier, it seemed to me that all I had thought about and was telling students, together with all that I had written, ought to be brought together in a book. Whilst the landscape planning committee of the IUCN had developed well, there still wasn't a basic document, so I produced a book called *Landscape Planning*. In it, I tried to show how a landscape plan could or ought to be applied to all forms of development and how it could have an ecological basis. Perhaps now I would like to rewrite it − a lot has happened since then − but I think it was possibly the first work on this subject, before McHarg's book was produced, so it was a pioneer work in that sense.

I have always been rather interested in planting design, trying to see whether one could produce planting designs which were based upon ecology but could still give room for the designer to adapt whatever was the natural approach to the particular problem he was having to deal with. So I thought over this and produced a course on the subject at the university, which was built up over the years and was adapted and improved. There were very few books that actually told the student how to relate this plant to that plant, either ecologically or visually. The only one that I ever came across was the two volumes of Professor Robinson's, produced years ago in the USA, which did treat the juxtaposition of plants as a design exercise, looking at the different attributes of plants and how they related together. The result of this was my book on *Planting Design*. Then also I was involved in either writing chapters of books or alternatively editing works on landscape reclamation which were the result of the vast landscape reclamation project that I administered at the university in Newcastle. And the last book produced was on the important topic of *Landscape Conservation*. We have after all got many beautiful areas in this country, either man-made or natural, but they are all subject to enormous pressures. We need to look at landscape conservation in terms of enabling landscapes to continue into the future; it is not just a matter of preservation like preserving buildings by repairing them, but of actually deciding how the landscape should be managed or modified to ensure its survival. How in fact can you keep a living thing alive which is constantly dying?

A society which throws out everything that has been developed in the past is making a big mistake. I think we can learn a lot from historical landscapes and, in many cases, they are the ones that we are not able to design today because of economic or land ownership reasons. Therefore we should at least preserve them as examples of an earlier kind of landscape design. I am not pessimistic about the future of the natural environment because there is such an enormous lobby all over the world for things of this nature. Take one example, the question of stubble burning has been the subject of letters to *The Times* and of a session of the 1983 Liberal Party Conference. This concern is worldwide; for example, the World Wildlife Fund, distinguished people like the Duke of Edinburgh getting involved, David Bellamy kicking up a fuss in Tasmania about the threatened flooding of a valley and getting success in the end. Now, although the level of change is tremendous, it is balanced by the enormous number of people acting in a very forthright manner for the good of the landscape in its wider sense.

Nevertheless, many third world countries feel that food comes before conservation and that they must have resource development and exploitation in order to survive. One way of looking at the problem is this: the developed countries of the world have developed into their present state of civilisation over approximately the last thousand years, while the undeveloped countries are having to undergo the same revolution in something like 50 years. We have to remember that we took a thousand years to change the landscape of what we now call the developed countries. Now morally it is difficult to say to the undeveloped countries 'you shouldn't be doing this, you are wrong': I know as a result of force of circumstances they are likely to create for themselves some terrific landscape problems, of erosion, of the imbalance of wildlife, causing certain plants to overdevelop, others to die out, and so on. I think that somehow we have got to persuade them to learn by our mistakes, that unless they are prepared to follow landscape planning principles, they will get into the same difficulties. There is an enormous problem in these countries and whether they will realise the difficulties or get sufficient political influence quickly enough to solve it, I don't know.

I was out in Ghana in 1975, where I was asked to talk about the ecological approach to landscape in one of the universities. During my time there a three-day symposium on landscape planning had been organised (which I masterminded) and we invited various forestry people, horticulturists, planners, anyone who might be concerned with the landscape, to come to it. They were very enthusiastic and eager to put these ideas into practice but Ghana was going through a very difficult political and economic situation at that time. So of course, these countries have a problem, and perhaps it is up to us to do something about it rather than to expect them to solve it on their own.

The Ecological Approach

There are two reasons why we should seriously consider an ecological approach to landscape and planting design. The first is that within the last few years a lot more land has been subjected to what we might call landscape design and landscape development and I would hope there is going to be more and more in the future. This is creating vast areas of land which, if developed like the Chelsea Flower Show or the nineteenth century public park, would be extremely costly in terms of staff to maintain. We have obviously to find some way of being able to look after these areas economically. We need to find a way of developing a landscape which can be more or less self-perpetuating; one of the ways to do this must surely be through research in the ecological field. The other comes back to what I said earlier: I believe that an association with a rich, full landscape where there are birds and animals, trees and shrubs, in other words a whole landscape, is a good thing. On social and moral grounds alone, I believe this to be a form of landscape and planting design which is worth exploring and developing in the future.

It would be a very good thing for students to see more of the economic benefits of what they are doing and perhaps also learn much more about birds and animals, either through zoology or natural history studies. One of my difficulties has always been teaching on either a one-year or a two-year course, which has made it difficult to get everything in! Through the ecological approach, we have endeavoured to get some appreciation of wildlife and how to provide suitable habitats for it, but we have been unable to go into any depth, such as one year of full-time study in a department of zoology would provide. On the other hand, I am also a great believer in self-education and I think that when a student leaves the university after a four-year or a two-year course he will go on learning if he is any good. These courses should provide the student with enough background and ideas to enable him to carry out his own research in the future.

The Landscape Institute

There is no doubt that the influence the Institute has had on environmental change in this country has been and is very considerable. Even if you measured it in terms of the number of hectares which have been the subject of landscape schemes, it would still be very considerable. Also the fact that landscape architects working in planning authorities and architectural offices are now having much more influence; their opinions are much more listened to than they used to be and this is a good thing. The Institute, I think, is probably suffering from one of the problems which all organisations suffer from as they get bigger – decentralisation. There used to be meetings in London at which there was always a speaker; he or she may have been a landscape architect or somebody from the outside, but this was a way of showing that the Institute was interested in the educational or cultural development of society in relation to landscape problems. Now, the Institute is simply the place where committee and Council meetings take place: business rather than discussions on the principles or problems of landscape design. Now the tendency is for the Chapters to hold these discussions and lectures, and I have a slight suspicion that they tend to become regional bodies and the cross fertilisation of ideas within the Institute as a whole is lost. There is now lacking a centre from which development in landscape culture, landscape research and so on can be put across both to members and a wider public.

The formation of the Chapters was a good development and was inevitable, and does mean that landscape architects in a particular region get plenty of opportunity to meet together and discuss things. But it can also, unless one is very careful, lead to too much decentralisation, too many separate bodies doing their own thing. The Institute's journal, *Landscape Design*, is I suppose now the medium for keeping the Institute together. It is a very good magazine and grows in popularity, but it does tend to concentrate on articles dealing with projects. Occasionally there is one on an historical aspect, but it does seem to lack the cultural background. To give a case in point, the old journal of the Institute of Landscape Architects, going back to the '30s, was much more the journal of an academic body. A professional institute needs to be academic as well as simply administrative and project-oriented, while also looking after the 'trade union' aspects of the profession; it would help if we could get some philosophical content back into the journal.

An important function of the Institute is to attempt to gain influence in the corridors of power, and on government and government legislation. Once upon a time, it was simply a question of having the right connections and knowing the right people; but to make an impact now at a political level often requires a lot of money and a lot of factual research. For example, if you are going to oppose an atomic power station, you can certainly go and say that it will spoil the appearance of the countryside or ruin a historic viewpoint, but really to make the point, you have to be conversant with the economic and safety problems as well. It would be very costly for the Institute to provide research or technical facilities on this scale. Another difficulty is that inevitably now many of the Institute's presidents are based in the provinces, as I was, and it is not so easy to cultivate the right contacts living away from London.

Fellow Professionals

During the course of my career I have met and benefited from associations with many landscape architects, some of whom have made outstanding contributions to the profession. Take Sir Geoffrey Jellicoe: his contributions were very very considerable, but there are three things which stand out in my mind. The first was his energy in the very early days, in the late 1920s and 1930s, in getting the Institute established, which in itself was a great achievement. Secondly, he got to know a number of important people and was able to do quite a lot for landscape by quiet lobbying with ministers and influential people, and had a great influence in that way. Thirdly, he was a man of most interesting aesthetic ideas. I don't know that all of them are strictly within the ecological approach to landscape, perhaps, but his forward-looking ideas, particularly in trying to relate landscape design to the other arts, were very stimulating. So, for me, those are the three things which stand out as his especial qualities. Another colleague was Brenda Colvin and to my mind her *Land and Landscape* was a pioneer book which had an enormous influence in spreading a wider view of landscape. She was very forthright, very outspoken and probably because of that did not advance as far as she might have done, so I was delighted when eventually she was given the CBE, because she was undoubtedly a pioneer. I can remember the late director of the Countryside Commission giving a paper at a landscape conference in Scotland, which showed some slight suspicion of landscape architects: Brenda Colvin got up and let him have it in no uncertain terms.

Then there was Sylvia Crowe. She and Brenda were very good friends and quite different personalities. Sylvia had the charm and ability to influence people; she had the ability to win people over. Brenda Colvin lacked that facility, although in my opinion she was just as good a landscape architect, but her personality was perhaps a little staccato and prevented her from creating for herself the same public opportunities.

I think that nowadays there are many very good landscape architects: one could almost say that they are two-a-penny, doing great projects all over the place, but going back to the early days of landscape design, I was always impressed by Peter Youngman's work. To my mind, he produced very good landscape designs without being at all flamboyant, which were always very well related to the site. Frank Clark never had enough opportunity in the designing field. At first there wasn't much opportunity for landscape work and then by the time there was, he had got involved with teaching in Edinburgh. He was, I would say, a very sensitive designer and was influenced by the historical approach to landscape design. His famous book brought a lot of people to understand that there was an English school of landscape. That was an artistic development, one of the few individualistic art developments of this country. I always say that the Perpendicular style of architecture, the English school of landscape, the musical development of the Elizabethan age and, shortly after that, the English school of watercolour, were the four major artistic achievements of this country. And Frank Clark's book brought a lot of people to realise that. I would say that quite a number of other books that have now been published on the English school of landscape, including American PhD studies, have probably resulted from the fact that Frank Clark made everyone realise that it was a definite art movement.

Observations
on Contemporary Design

The New Town landscapes were a great achievement and something which other countries have flocked to see. I suppose that Cumbernauld at one time was held up as being the great example, but Milton Keynes is the greater landscape achievement, largely because it was the last one and therefore could learn from the mistakes of previous new towns; and also because it was given an enormous area of land and was able to do a lot of tree planting in what were (and probably still are) agricultural areas. So there was a landscape foundation planting of thousands of trees, which I imagine must give by now a very settled appearance to the town.

Another example I remember was Sir Geoffrey Jellicoe's landform design for a large brewery in north London[6]. That was a fairly pioneer landform design and was about the same time that the Institute was trying to decide what papers might be given at future meetings. I suggested that we ought to have papers which looked at new approaches to landscape design, actually going into the basic problems and theory. The result was that I presented a paper in 1959 called 'Basic Design and Landform' in which I tried to find some principles of landform design. This was partly sparked off by Jellicoe's brewery work and, of course, vast landform projects have been done since then.

The reshaping of spoil heaps can be seen as an aesthetic exercise; with these schemes, it is possible to create a new kind of outdoor sculpture, some of which is good and some bad, but we learn from solving problems. Just to give one case in point, on the Town Moor in Newcastle, they have now got a vast inverted saucer which came from the excavations of the urban motorway. I always pointed out to students that this was how not to deal with it, because it is an artificial landform in a very large landscape. In my opinion, there is a certain size of landscape beyond which you can't have this artificial sculpture effect; it doesn't look right.

I suppose that hard landscape had never been much more than an extension of architecture. For example, even in a Lutyens garden, the hard landscape was really an extension of the architecture. The landscape profession has made quite a large contribution here, for example, Tommy Church's work in America; he produced hard landscape design which you couldn't trace back to any building architectural background. In fact, I think that his hard landscape designs stemmed largely from working with the soft landscape; he was the pioneer of the contemporary landscape design movement in the USA. There are, of course, many plaza and mall developments in the United States, many of which could not have been done in this country – they were too expensive. I find them a bit over-sophisticated; they are rather like some of the plaza designs which were done in Italy in the sixteenth and seventeenth centuries. To my mind, it is a pity that there is so much hard landscape and not enough green landscape, which perhaps we don't need from an aesthetic point of view but I think we need green landscape so that man can have a closer relationship with nature.

An International Outlook

I suppose I was both fortunate from my own point of view and it was perhaps fortunate for the Institute of Landscape Architects in this country, that I got invited to a very large number of countries by various universities, for the most part to introduce the idea of the ecological and landscape planning approaches to design, and even to the extent of being invited to speak to Forestry and Housing conferences – not specifically landscape conferences. I think this was a very useful thing because it spread knowledge about the Institute and encouraged a number of people to come to this country as students, providing valuable intercommunication and spreading of ideas.

Some of my students have gone back to their country of origin and have become quite well known and influential people, so that the ecological approach to landscape design is now international. It doesn't matter whether you are working in the desert or in Greenland, or in the middle of Russia, the ecological approach is equally relevant. Obviously, the result looks different in each country, because if you follow ecological principles faithfully, you will take into account the natural conditions of the country in which you are working, but the basic approach should be the same wherever you are. There is too the International Federation of Landscape Architects but this is a bit limited by the fact that the number of people who can afford to attend large international conferences is fairly small.

One of the ways in which the landscape profession can develop a more international outlook with a corresponding exchange of knowledge and ideas is by practice in other countries. An exchange of students is another possibility which could be explored and there should be a greater exchange of young people working in landscape offices. For example, if a big landscape firm in London was employing 20 assistants, they could send one of their assistants to work in a practice in say Hong Kong for a year, with a chap from Hong Kong coming to work in London. An exchange at that level would provide particularly good experience.

The Future of the Profession

Landscape design or architecture is a very fascinating profession. Just looking at it as a job of work, you get chances of going out from the office into different parts of the region or the country, an opportunity to do something creative, and you are always meeting interesting people; landscape colleagues always seem to be nice people – the profession seems to attract them. It seems to me that a lot of children have seen what a pleasant, interesting and full life it offers[7], and also it does match well with the present social and environmental concern of young people. Students coming into the profession today are given a much better technical background than I ever had – they haven't got to go through all the hard job of self-learning – and they have a much better opportunity of progressing more quickly than I or some of the pioneers of the Institute had. The landscape profession does meet social, ecological and environmental objectives and I think many people are today concerned about the world they live in. The landscape profession offers them a constructive opportunity to do something about it.

Notes

1   Thomas Jeffryes, architect and planner, married Jane Wood in 1953. Jane joined the Landscape Institute in 1949 and, encouraged by her husband, developed a successful practice in Edinburgh and became a fellow of the Institute.
2   Thomas Mawson (1861–1933) was first president of the then Institute of Landscape Architects, although failing health prevented him from taking an active part in its activities. A biographical article was published in *Landscape Design* in August 1979, pp.30–33, written by his grandson, the architect David Mawson.
3   Lord Eustace Percy was the son of the 7th Duke of Northumberland and had been Minister of Education for a period during the 1930s.
4   H.F. Clark, president of the ILA from 1959 to 1961, whose educational posts included a part-time lectureship in the Department of Fine Art at Reading, first postwar lecturer in landscape in the Department of Civic Design at Liverpool, and senior landscape lecturer in the Department of Architecture at Edinburgh.
5   The Tennessee Valley Authority was established by the US government in the 1930s to replan a vast region which had become a dust bowl as a result of overcropping.
6   The Guinness 'Hills' – see chapter on Sir Geoffrey Jellicoe.
7   Professor Hackett's son Nigel C. Hackett also became a landscape architect and is, at the time of writing, an associate of Derek Lovejoy & Partners, seconded to Urbis in Hong Kong.

Peter Youngman

Peter Youngman has a degree in history from Cambridge University and is a fellow of both the Royal Town Planning Institute and the Landscape Institute. His work has been divided between private practice and education, mainly as part time teacher at University College London from 1948 to 1978, latterly as the first visiting professor in landscape design. He was president of the Landscape Institute from 1961 to 1963 and was awarded the CBE in 1983.

Early Life

I was born in Leeds in 1911 and three years later went to live at Hartlepool on the Durham coast. My father was a bank manager and we lived there until he retired when I was 18.

I don't remember anything about Leeds; but I recall very well the house we lived in on the edge of Hartlepool (the then edge), with fields on one side and a farm not far away. The house had been built, I suppose, around 1900 – a middle class family home, not very large but with a garden of an acre and a half or so. A very dull, utilitarian garden: a shrubbery with trees and some beds of asters and geraniums in the front; a gravel drive up to the front door and round to a stable at the back; lawns at the back, one of which we played badminton on and the other croquet; a small orchard, with rough grass, to one side and a tiny flower garden behind that; the rest was vegetables and fruit. No aesthetic design whatsoever. My mother looked after the flower garden, but my father did nothing at all. We used to have a man who came several days a week, who cut the grass, weeded the drive and grew the vegetables. I had my own little garden as a child.

We didn't travel a great deal and we hadn't a car (not many people had when I was a boy). I suppose that I only became aware of the landscape when I went away to school at Worksop. That was a very Philistine school and I wasn't particularly happy there. It may have had some influence on my choice of career in that the school lay between Welbeck on the west and Clumber on the east and both of these parks we boys had access to. On half holidays and at weekends I used to go for walks in these, without any idea of their significance, nor with anybody at school knowing about it either; but the park landscapes and the woods were there for me to see, and I enjoyed that. Nor was there anyone at school to rouse an interest in nature study. Nor did any of my relatives or family friends know much about the birds and butterflies and flowers, or have any interest in rural life. Even though my father's family had all been country dwellers and farming people, he and all his brothers went into business, largely because my grandfather was a failure as a farmer.

At school I was best at what I took Higher Certificate in, which was history. I had more interest in that than classics or languages which were the other possibilities. At maths I was hopeless and science I scarcely ever did, even in the early years. Science (i.e. physics and chemistry only) was still something of a novelty, much looked down on by the traditionalists. My last three years at school were spent almost exclusively on history, for the Higher Certificate and for university scholarship. I only got an exhibition; but that meant history was my subject at Cambridge.

While at school I had been on camping trips in France and Belgium and Switzerland. While an undergraduate I spent a month one summer in Scandinavia and another in Austria. I enjoyed the scenery and the mountain walking and the music at Salzburg; and the gardens of Schloss Hellbrunn outside Salzburg. Also I was beginning to be aware of architecture, not only historic buildings but the new railway station at Helsinki and the town hall at Stockholm.

Early Influences and Apprenticeships

I don't know what brought me into landscape architecture. There was certainly no outside influence, no person who could set an example or talk to me about it. It came about in the latter part of my second year at Cambridge, having to think about what sort of job I should go for and not particularly attracted to any of the things that a history degree might have led to – teaching, administration or civil service. I would have liked to have been an academic, but my intellectual calibre was too low. At that time what mainly directed my thoughts was a determination to do something that would be worthwhile and enjoyable rather than just earn a living; even though (my father had by then died) my uncles were urging me to look for a safe job in business or in a bank.

I had always enjoyed gardening as a small boy at Hartlepool, as I did when my mother, after my father had died, got a small house in Surrey. So it seemed that something to do with gardening might suit me, perhaps also something to do with garden designing. I remember seeing *Country Life* with its pictures and plans of country houses and their gardens and its gardening articles; and that may have given me the idea. Nobody at Cambridge could help; they all thought it a waste of a good university education. But I was given a few introductions – to the then director of Kew, to Robert Wallace of the big firm of nurserymen and garden contractors in Tunbridge Wells, to the gardening editor of *Country Life*. But nothing came of these. Then somebody suggested I wrote to one of the garden contracting firms to ask if they could do anything for me. So out of the blue I wrote to Whiteleggs of Chislehurst, which was not too far away from where I lived. I had discovered their renown as exhibitors at the Chelsea Flower Show and Ideal Homes Exhibition, especially for rock gardens (which had long taken my fancy). They offered to take me as an apprentice, charge £50 a year as a premium and pay it back as weekly pocket money. So for a year I worked in the nursery, on the stands at the shows and with the men making rockeries and lily ponds, laying crazy paving and planting suburban gardens. This was quite strenuous physically, but no doubt a good antidote to the sheltered academic life, especially alongside the Cockney workmen, who quickly took the mickey out of me. Though once I learnt the slang and could join in repartee, they became very friendly and readily taught me their skills. Except for one surly old man they did not grudge (or at least not outwardly) my obviously privileged position. As an early influence they were by no means the least.

This experience left me feeling that I did not want to go on in the commercial world but all the more strongly that I wanted to be a garden designer; and to do that it was clear that I must learn to draw, if only a plan. I had never had any inclination to draw or paint (and am still no good at sketching); but I tried to learn from the draughtsman in the Whitelegg office who produced the firm's very crude designs. And I attended a term of evening classes at the Bromley Art School, which was nearby; but I didn't get much out of that. So I began to realise I needed to work with a garden designer. Through a friend I was introduced to George Dillistone, then (this was 1935) the vice-president of the tiny but developing Institute of Landscape Architects. He had been the designer for Wallace's but was then with his own practice, working from his home in Tunbridge Wells, with one assistant, a technical chap who did his surveys and drawings and specifications. He agreed to take me as an articled pupil, charging a premium but paying it back as pocket money. So for two years I went to work there, travelling daily from Oxted. I didn't learn a great deal from him. His designing was competent but uninspiring: herbaceous borders, rose gardens, yew hedges, dry stone walls, wrought iron gates, in a feeble Lutyens–Jekyll idiom. In this way I acquired some skill in producing garishly coloured drawings, in drawing up planting plans, in very simple surveys and setting out, and some experience of supervising jobs; but no experience of contracts. He used to engage foremen (he had a couple of regulars) and workmen on his client's behalf and act as the clients' agent and supervisor.

My gradual learning about design and about plants, soils and so on was pretty haphazard. I was beginning to read books, but in those days there were so few, even on horticulture. Some catalogues were informative. I remember particularly a huge and lavishly illustrated volume produced by a long since defunct firm called Gauntlett: a snobbishly exclusive firm doing business only with the very wealthy or aristocratic. On plants and planting design there were the Jekyll and Robinson books, and various monographs, like Farrer on alpine plants, or Dykes on irises (Dillistone was an iris enthusiast and a leading light in the Iris Society).

On landscape design there was an utterly useless book by Richard Sudell, the enormous volume of Thomas Mawson's *Art and Craft of Garden Making* (which I soon began to find too olde-worlde) a *Country Life* book on Lutyen's houses and gardens and another called *Garden Ornament*, and a reprint of text and photographs from the periodical. Also from *Country Life* was Laurence Weaver's *Gardens for Small Country Houses*. Of these, Mawson's I found encouraging because it showed somebody actually practising the professional skill I was aiming at. It was instructive in a practical way too. Above all were Geoffrey Jellicoe's two historical works – *Garden Design* and *Gardens of the Italian Renaissance*. These opened my eyes to garden design as a creative art; and that I realised I cared about most of all. The Italian book also taught me the importance of the cross-section. It reveals the third dimension, accurately, precisely, measurable in a way no perspective sketch ever can. When plan and section are well proportioned there is a sure basis for a good design. Aesthetically good I mean; but there are many other criteria a design has to satisfy.

Introduction to Town Planning

When I was with Dillistone I began to be aware of landscape as countryside and not just parks and gardens. It was a time when Clough Williams-Ellis and others were writing polemical books (such as *Britain and the Beast*) and the Council for the Preservation of Rural England was increasingly active. People were becoming conscious of the damage being done to the rural landscape – ribbon development, trunk roads, advertisement hoardings, caravans. It seemed to me that designing herbaceous borders for Surrey and Sussex stockbrokers would scarcely be a worthwhile lifetime occupation. There were bigger concerns, more public. Through Dillistone I had come to know about the ILA and I began to see its journal. I noticed that among its small body of members were town planners, not only architects and garden designers.

I was introduced through friends to Prentice Mawson, who spanned all these activities. One of the sons of Thomas Mawson, he was a trained architect and town planner and was carrying on his father's practice. A bluff but genial north countryman, he was very helpful and encouraging and let me see what was going on in his office. By him I was introduced to Thomas Adams and to a complete reorientation of my career.

Thomas Adams was then president of the ILA, a great support in those early formative years. He was a surveyor in his original profession and one of the founders of the Town Planning Institute. In a way it is a misnomer to call him a landscape architect. He had never himself done any landscape designing (or any other kind of designing for that matter, even though he was FRIBA); and I don't remember him doing any drawing. But he had an awareness of the role of the landscape architect and an appreciation of its professional value, derived from his experience in the USA. At the time I was introduced to him he had recently returned from having been for seven years director of a regional plan for New York. That must have been one of the biggest planning projects of its time in the whole of the world. How he got the job I haven't the slightest idea; but it meant he was coordinating the work of many different professions, among them landscape architects. He would have known of the American park planning tradition going back to Olmsted; of the landscape school at Harvard; of a profession already well established. This was a profession already concerned with much more than gardens; and was much more like that of town planning in this country. I imagine Adams saw himself in that light rather than as a small-scale landscape designer.

My introduction to him came at a lucky moment. He was establishing himself again as a planning consultant in London and was looking round for staff to help him. He was still precarious professionally, so he wasn't wanting a large office or well qualified people. He was happy to take on myself and another chap of about my own age as sort of trainee assistants, paying just about enough to cover travelling expenses and pocket money. So I had a spell of nearly three years with him. During this time I was elected an associate of the Institute on the strength of a meagre set of drawings, far below present-day examination standards.

Adams had a Scots dourness, but he could be genial; and he was very kind to me in a fatherly sort of way. He must have been in his late 60s. He wasn't very cultured and not in the slightest degree artistic. I doubt whether he was musical, nor was he at all philosophical or widely read outside his professional field. Yet he produced a book *Outline of Town and City Planning*, which was largely historical and very fully researched. And, clearly, he had mastered the skills of a planning consultant of that period, though not of a calibre to match Raymond Unwin or Patrick Abercrombie. When I was with him he was consultant to the Thames Valley Regional Planning Committee and the West Middlesex Planning Committee, so he was giving a modicum of planning oversight to all that was happening west of London as far as Windsor. It is a sad commentary on the efficacy of our planning system to see what has happened, around Heathrow for example, in the 50 years since his regime. He was also preparing planning maps under the 1932 Town Planning Act for the boroughs of Bexhill, Hastings and Walthamstow. A large part of my time was spent in the careful colouring of these 1:2500 ordnance maps. These would (it seems incredible when one looks back at the system as it was then), once they had been approved by the councils, have been submitted to parliament for ratification; would then have had the force of law and been almost unalterable. Not surprisingly, no such plans ever reached the final stage; the war put them into limbo, and the 1947 Act abolished the unwieldy procedure. It meant that most of my time was spent just in being accurate, being careful where my brush put a bit of green or a bit of purple so that I did not zone some industrialist's land as open space and vice versa. The content of the plans was extremely naive and banal.

Soon after I arrived in the office Tom Jeffryes (Jane Wood's husband – see note 1 of Brian Hackett's chapter) joined the firm. He was the first architect I had ever met. He not only taught me a lot about architecture as such, but also about design as an activity common to both professions. He made me aware of the basic things like proportion, scale and function. 'Form follows function' was one of the contemporary catchwords. I owe a great debt to Tom; as I do to so many of the architects I have worked with since those days, who have in effect been my design tutors. During this time I was fortunate enough to meet Christopher Tunnard, whose *Gardens in the Modern Landscape* opened a new world for me, and Frank Clark who was by then working as his assistant. Tunnard would talk knowledgeably and enthusiastically about Corbusier and Bauhaus and contemporary art. I didn't understand much, but found it far, far more exciting than Mawson or even Lutyens (who was taboo to those for whom 'Corb' was the hero).

Education as a Planner

Adams was giving some lectures at a planning school in Bedford Square and told me to go and talk with E.A.A. Rowse who had very recently started it up. Rowse was then head of the Architectural Association school of architecture, and as an offshoot of that had organised this part-time postgraduate evening course in planning studies. It soon became independent. Rowse was at loggerheads with the AA Council (his sort of planning was not the traditional civic design that they understood) and resigned. He was the sort of farsighted person that ordinary people label a crank, and was propounding all sorts of later commonplaces of postwar thinking: that architecture was not just about individual buildings but part of town planning; that town planning was much more than civic design, more than a concern with buildings and roads, piazzas and parks; that (he being a disciple of Patrick Geddes) planning was concerned with people and places, with home and work, with food, recreation, travel and transport; that all these interlocked and had to be planned for jointly, in the first instance nationally and regionally and thence down to the locality. Tom Jeffryes was his deputy and my studio teacher. I don't recall many of the lecturers; but Jellicoe talked to us about landscape – it was the first time I had heard of Le Nôtre and Capability Brown. And we were lucky enough to have Raymond Unwin. He was the foremost planner of his time: short, not very impressive physically, but bubbling with enthusiasm, full of ideas, very stimulating. Rowse himself gave the history lectures, and intrigued me by starting with the familiar present and tracing its roots in the unfamiliar past; and captivating me with his synoptic view of world history. Cambridge had had nothing to say to me about Egypt, India, China, or the origins of civilisation or prehistoric man.

There were few text books. For all the talk of Geddes I did not read any of his writings. I don't recall any being readily available. But there was Lewis Mumford's (he being the most influential of Geddes' disciples) *Culture of Cities*, hot from the press. The other bible for me (though it came too late to influence Rowse and the other students, and perhaps was too technical anyway) was Tansley's *The British Islands and their Vegetation*, which appeared in 1939. There was Raymond Unwin's *Town Planning in Practice*, the exposition of his ideas and experience of garden city designing. And I recall Thomas Sharp's two books, *English Panorama* and *Town and Countryside.* Sharp was an outspoken character, with strong convictions and somewhat irascible temper. At that time he was putting the cat among the professional pigeons by attacking the prevailing orthodoxy of garden city low-density development, demonstrating the qualities of traditional urbanity, even the urban character of many a village. These, and his postwar planning reports on Oxford (this one especially), Salisbury and Chichester taught me much. Particularly he taught me to see, literally to see, to appreciate and take a delight in the urban scenery of pre-industrial towns and cities, the strong antithesis between town and country.

Rowse – it was typical of his catholic attitude – welcomed me as a budding landscape architect. But I was not the only one. Jackie Tyrwhitt (already a qualified member of the Institute) was my contemporary as a student. She became a great Geddes disciple, a firm believer in planning regionally, over geographical rather than local authority areas; and in comprehensive survey and analysis before plan (commonplace now, but not to civic designers then). She revived the school after the war and more or less took over its running. She was too energetic, too forceful and full of ideas not to be in charge, and by then Rowse's interests had become international. He faded from the scene, but was heard of for a while as adviser to the Emperor of Ethiopia. Rowse and Tyrwhitt had a great and personal influence on many postwar planners, particularly those who were students on their refresher courses for demobilised servicemen.

I spent two years at this school, and got my diploma just before the outbreak of war. That let me into the Town Planning Institute, though somewhat *sub rosa*. It being a postgraduate course one was supposed to have a relevant professional qualification. Only three at that time mattered to the Institute – architecture, engineering and surveying. Landscape architecture hadn't been heard of. History was too academic. But somehow, on the score of both these and the diploma, Rowse wheedled it for me. Incidentally I know of only two other landscape architects (Paul Edwards and Michael Tooby) who have gone on to qualify for the TPI.

The Second World War

I volunteered for the Army a few weeks after the outbreak of the war, and served first in the medical corps and then in the infantry, for most of the time in England and Northern Ireland.

During the months of the 'phoney war' I continued reading when I had the time; the Mumford and Tansley volumes – both their titles and their bulk – at the bottom of my army locker caused some amazement during barrack room inspections. But once the war got going in earnest, with the German occupation of Europe and the blitzes in this country, creative interests seemed pointless, heartless too. So professionally there was a six-year hiatus – though not entirely without some later benefit. On intelligence and staff courses I got a rigorous training in orderly thinking, in clear analysis of purposes and means. At corps headquarters I had experience of interdisciplinary collaboration. My postings took me to Egypt, Palestine, Italy and Austria. And right at the end I was sent back to Salerno for a month while waiting my turn to be demobbed, with a final ten day's leisurely journey through Rome and Florence to Milan and the train home to 'civvy street'. That was a marvellous and eye-opening experience which I was then in a mood to enjoy: the Mediterranean landscape, harbour towns, olive groves and cypresses, brilliant light, transparent sea; the famous buildings and piazzas of the cities; opera in Naples and Rome; no tourists or traffic anywhere. And my first chance to see some of the gardens: Caserta, then Alexander's HQ, ponderous and dull; the Villa Medici above the Spanish Steps in Rome, austere and secluded; one of the villas outside Florence where the elderly owner remembered well Jellicoe's visit and turned up the description and illustration in his book; above all the Villa Gamberaia near Florence, the gardens neglected and unkempt, the house damaged by fire when the Germans retreated, but the subtle geometry of the design immensely exciting.

Post-War Years

On coming out of the Army in 1945 I had two possibilities. As a qualified member of two institutes I could have looked for a job as a town planner or as a landscape architect. Being undecided I went to ask the advice of Geoffrey Jellicoe, whom I had met before the war. I owe a very great debt to him, as do so many others personally, as we all do corporately for what he did to keep the Institute together during and after the war. With his typical enthusiasm he said to me, 'There is a great future for landscape architects. There are very few and there is much work to be done. Get yourself a room, a drawing board, some headed notepaper and start'. That was exactly what I wanted to hear. I really wanted to be a designer rather than a planner, though I hoped I could be more than a garden designer. Not only did Geoffrey give me that direct encouragement, but he also said he had been offered a job that he had not time for. I suspect he was saying so to give me a helping hand, but that introduced me to a client who helped to set me on my feet and to a group of architects who introduced me to contemporary architecture, whom I had briefly met before the war when they were still students at the Architectural Association. They were the group who became Architects Co-partnership, leading architects of their generation (with whom I worked a few years later on the 1951 South Bank Exhibition). Then they were working on a very *avant-garde* building – a rubber factory – in South Wales, with Ove Arup as consulting engineer. The client was Jim Forrester, the elder son of the then Earl of Verulam who became Earl of Verulam in due course. He was a friend also of Rowse and Tyrwhitt and a supporter of their school of planning.

Forrester was managing director of an industrial firm in Enfield, and it was an offshoot of that firm that he was establishing in Brynmawr. Little came of the work I did there. Much of it was woodland on a derelict coal tip. Fire destroyed some of the trees; sheep devoured the rest. When the factory ran into production trouble soon after the start, it was taken over by Dunlop, and Forrester lost control. But he had many other interests and over several years produced a variety of small jobs for me. The last of these, and the best, was the conversion of a derelict old graveyard close to the cathedral at St Albans. That, surprisingly, has survived largely intact: no floribunda roses, as so frequently elsewhere, have been added; and the rough mown grass remains, as the only example of this that I have been able to achieve other than in my own garden. This scheme, completed in 1951, was the first contract I had had to specify and supervise. All the other work for Forrester was by direct labour.

Landscape Design Education

Forrester thus helped me to establish a small private practice, but the income was only a few hundred a year, so I was very pleased when opportunities to teach came my way. First was at the Rowse/Tyrwhitt school, where (together with Brian Hackett, whom I met for the first time) I was helping with project work for the planning students, but very soon I was providing lectures and studio instruction specifically intended for landscape architects. Mary Mitchell and Zvi Miller were among those early students. After that came a part-time job at the then Regent Street Polytechnic, with lectures on landscape and planning history and studio instruction for planning students. Then, after the ILA had raised the money to fund two teaching developments, the first at Newcastle (where Brian Hackett was appointed) and the second at University College London, I was lucky enough to get the part-time lectureship there under Bill Holford. That academic start was a great reassurance in terms of livelihood and family responsibilities. It meant I could persist in a landscape career rather than having to fall back on a job in a local authority planning department.

The college at that time provided a part-time evening course in planning for postgraduate students, so Holford suggested I set up something similar for people who might be interested in landscape design. But it was a very much smaller affair. There was little finance other than the grant for my salary, and I had to do most of the teaching myself, though with some help from the staff at Wye College. As for syllabus, I had to invent that. The experience of the course under Jackie Tyrwhitt was a bit of a guide, and I could consult with my nearest academic colleague Frank Clark. At the end of the war he had been appointed to take charge of the landscape course, at Reading, and later to the first lectureship at Liverpool. At Reading there was a full-time undergraduate course, a hybrid between the departments of art and horticulture, which were often at loggerheads with each other, causing considerable difficulties for Frank. He himself was much more attuned to fine art than horticulture; ineffective as a practitioner (and with little opportunity, as a full-time teacher, to practice) but a sensitive historian and an elegant writer, and a great stimulus to his students, both at Reading and later at Edinburgh, who had a great affection for him. But his regime at Reading was not directly relevant to what I was having to do at University College. His course was full-time and undergraduate; mine was part-time and postgraduate.

Twenty years or so later came the development of the now well established undergraduate and postgraduate courses at universities and polytechnics. Without them the profession could never have expanded so largely and so rapidly. How long can they viably continue? For how long will students leaving a course be sure of getting a job? Who can foresee? But some time there must come a slowing down, and with that some reorganisation of courses. I think it better that there should continue to be as many schools as can attract a viable intake of students (say 15–20) than a concentration into a few large establishments. I would like, too, a greater diversity in the character of courses, deriving from their situation or the special interests of their staff, with students enabled, in fact encouraged, to change from one to another for their final year. Looking further ahead, when the fully professional courses shrink; when continuing education is seen as one of the alternatives to the wasteful idleness of conventional unemployment and universities and polytechnics are not so starved of funds, may there not be new opportunities for landscape design teaching? Already there are inputs to courses for architects, engineers, planners, parks' managers: why not for foresters, ecologists, farmers, gardeners, quantity surveyors, accountants and business managers? Why not in fact to students of all kinds, however briefly? Landscape is a reflection of all human activities. Everyone is affected by its future. Landscape design embraces a far wider range of topics than any other discipline (which is its particular difficulty, both in the learning and in the practice). Could it not become one of the synthesising studies, helping to break down the rigid barriers of our narrow academic specialisms? There could be great scope for part-time teaching/part-time practice, or for peripatetic teachers moving from one department to another.

In the years just after the war I had a share in the drafting of the Institute's first examination syllabus. Somewhat tentative and skimpy at first, it soon developed into more or less its present format. Thirty years or so is much too long to go unchanged; but I don't underestimate the task of revision. I can well remember the close scrutiny given to every word, the difficulties in getting committee members to agree. That syllabus included the obvious subjects like history, design, plants and soils, but also – and this was new – ecology, which was largely due to the influence of Brenda Colvin, Sylvia Crowe and Brian Hackett. It makes me smile today when people talk about a new approach to landscape design and the profound importance of ecology, and I hark back to what these three were advocating in the late 1940s, to what Brian Hackett was teaching at Newcastle. One weakness of the syllabus, now obvious, was its lack of emphasis on people. All professions have found this, and they all now seem much more ready to see themselves as the servants rather than the directors of the community. How one should cope with this academically I am not sure. Certainly I have little faith, from experience so far, in lectures by psychologists or sociologists, and I would not want to make students read the sort of journalistic verbiage that has come my way. Maybe, as with so much in our field, more is to be learnt from direct observation than from book learning and academic theorising. I am a great believer in outdoor teaching, in the ambulatory seminar.

I don't think it was sufficiently realised within the Institute that there is a great distinction between the format of examining set up for students working on their own, to be examined within the resources of a professional institute, and the sort of curriculum which should be established in a university or polytechnic, where teachers are the examiners and know their students personally. I have sensed too great a constraint imposed on modes of teaching because of requiring from recognised courses a close conformity with the Institute's own syllabus. Some diversity between courses is to be encouraged. Certainly if it had been possible to set up an undergraduate course at UCL that would have had to be different, because of the very nature of the college's course unit system. I also sense too great a rigidity and over-concern with minutiae in course documents, far too much time spent in staff discussions, too much paper being circulated. Courses must be coherently structured and must cover the generally accepted basic subjects, but that is no guarantee of success. What matters much more is the interaction between teachers and students, among the students themselves, and above all the enthusiasm they engender in each other.

It has been suggested that the present courses, reflecting the Institute syllabus, do not deal sufficiently with the great conservation issues that affect the landscapes of the world; that landscape architects should comprehend the risks of environmental deterioration or disaster (whatever those terms might mean) and should be taught how to cope with 'threatened landscapes'. That there are worldwide worries of much higher priority than the niceties of a science park or a housing layout is obvious; but desertification, destruction of rain forests, acid rain and the like are extremely complex problems – ecological problems but arising out of social, economic and political malfunctioning. In the first instance they need a plan, not a design; and I doubt if landscape designers can do much to help, until the solutions become small scale and localised. These problems are much more the concern of our scientist members, and as for their training I have not the knowledge or experience to make any suggestions. To make landscape designer students aware of these concerns is one thing – they will probably do it for themselves anyway; but to insert special studies into their courses is quite another. Students have far too much to contend with as it is, and I would always be seeking ways of paring down syllabuses. But in this general context I recall advice given to an annual conference of the Institute in Edinburgh some 20 odd years ago by Robert Grieve. He was for many years the leading planner in Scotland, took great interest in and gave great encouragement to our small but growing profession. 'Don't get too big for your boots', he said. I echo that. He had in mind maybe the self-seeking corporate egotism that at times mars every profession. But knowing him, I think he was warning also against too far-ranging and ambitious idealism. All students have visions of better worlds. It is a subtle task for teachers to nurture that idealism while tempering it with realism.

Institute Affairs

My two years (1961–63) as president were a natural extension of what I had been doing since 1946. Having served on committees, been honorary secretary and treasurer I was the next senior person available. I had no urge to develop anything new. The Institute's activities had been given a shape and direction. I saw my task as developing these, keeping the machinery of the Institute active and effective rather than launching out in new directions. I was all the time conscious of our slender resources – few members and little income. It seemed to me (and it still does) that the Institute's main task was to produce practitioners known to be qualified and found to be reliable. Propaganda for the cause of 'fine landscape' and promotion of the profession were secondary.

And qualified practitioners were more and more needed. Though there was a limit to what the Institute as such could do, much was being done by individuals in positions of influence. For example Holford had been appointed a part-time member of the Central Electricity Generating Board (CEGB). From that time no power station project was without a landscape architect; Sylvia Crowe made a pioneering, though still somewhat tentative, input at Bradwell. There were the ILA representatives on the Ministry of Transport advisory committee; and from that influence came the appointment of Michael Porter and the gradual build-up of the landscape section under him. In local authorities Adams in Kent, Atkinson in Durham, Oxenham in Suffolk were setting a lead in the counties. Others, like Laurie in Southampton, were finding niches in the boroughs. Demand was being generated for more professionals than were available, and a clearer need for more, preferably full-time, schools. Yet still the profession was relatively unknown. Few people had heard of, let alone met, a landscape architect.

In the '70s came the transformation into the Landscape Institute with its three classes of members – designers, managers and scientists. It took, as I recall, five or six years of preparation and discussion, generating much conflict of opinion. Original proposals for a fourth class – landscape planners – were soon dropped. Nobody could define a distinctive role with separate expertise. I supported the idea on the whole. Landscape architects were undoubtedly being required to undertake too many differing activities, demanding too great a range of skills. My chief uncertainty – and it remains – was whether enough people would be attracted to make the divisions effective. I can see scientists having a useful role, both as supporters of designers and in their own right; and have experienced this at Sizewell Nuclear Power Station where Dr Derek Ranwell is the board's ecological adviser. What I don't know from any personal contact is how the landscape managers are faring. I have no doubt that they could develop a role in their own right, especially in the countryside where myriad small changes in the landscape need guiding with a sensitive eye, through instructions on the site rather than a designer's drawing. Also designers should welcome managers whose advice they can call on, who will be sympathetic to designer's intentions, who will nurture their schemes to mature fruition. Sympathy is the key. Will it always be forthcoming? Unsatisfactory maintenance has been one of the profession's frequent complaints in the past. Not always inadequate maintenance, nor technical incompetence, but reflecting different attitudes and likings. When floribunda roses and neat grass are preferred to native shrubs and wild flower meadows, what is a contemporary designer to do? To provide each in appropriate places may be too simplistic an answer; and in any case tastes change, and many a landscape design has a long life span. It is tempting for designers to go their own way – indeed in so far as they are artists they will rightly want to. Managers are likely to be in closer touch with the public, and in this sphere too they could become our advisers.

Sub-Regional Planning Projects

During the 1960s many regional planning studies were carried out by British firms of planning consultants both in this country and abroad. I worked on several of these as a co-consultant with three firms, Colin Buchanan, Shankland/Cox and Llewellyn-Davies. Abroad were Kuwait, Nairobi, Kingston (Jamaica), Arras and Hvar/Orebic on the Adriatic coast of Yugoslavia. At home were the South Hampshire, Ashford, Deeside and Roskill Commission 3rd London Airport studies. There is little of that sort of work nowadays. I doubt what we did abroad has had much lasting effect, but for me it was intensely interesting and enjoyable (and altogether unanticipated), all the more so as the official journeys could be broken or economically extended. In these places landscape evaluation is not far removed from touristic sightseeing, but more purposeful and concentrated; and landscape surveys bring one into touch with local people and ways of life more than being a mere tourist can ever do. And what a spectacular range of landscapes these travels encompassed: deserts, with camels and

Bedouin flocks and sandstorms; coconut and orange groves, tea plantations, vineyards, lavender fields and aromatic maquis; tropical seas and beaches (sometimes, but not always, the pure white of travel brochures); African game parks and wild animals. And what an architectural range too: the monuments of Washington and the skyscrapers of New York; the acropolis of Athens; the mosques, great maidan and bazaar of Isfahan; the Kabaka's tomb in Kampala; the Italianate harbour towns of the Adriatic coast – Split, Hvar, Korcula and Dubrovnik (in Split our office was in a remnant of Diocletian's palace); but also the rural shacks of Kingston's hinterland, the shanty towns of Nairobi and (altogether unexpected) of Kuwait, the penurious peasant cottages of Yugoslavia.

At home two of the projects were abortive – there was no bridge over the Dee estuary, there was no airport on any of the four Roskill sites; and the South Hampshire study was superseded by a structure plan (more mundane but politically more realistic) prepared by the county and the two borough councils. This was the most comprehensive of the three, and, like them, government-sponsored. South Hampshire was an obvious area of growth. What size should that be, where should it be located, what form should it take? And what would be the effect on the New Forest?

My contribution to the study took the form of travelling round the countryside on my own (storing up the general characteristics in my memory rather than copiously annotating plans) and with other members of the team, talking with them, writing memoranda, influencing their thinking rather than taking over a specific section of the report. In this sort of study I have always been against the notion of a separate landscape plan. Landscape is implicit in the general master plan; landscape considerations influence many items in the written report; references to landscape occur naturally in many sections. My main task (as in the other studies) was to help establish where development should not take place. We found a clear boundary where the chalk ended and the tertiary sands and gravels began, topographically distinct on the ground and defined on the geological and contour plans. The chalkland was much more productive farmland and much grander scenery. To exclude it from development was an obvious decision. Between that line and the sea, there were some obvious places for regional parks (woodlands, country houses and river meadows) which might be delimited at the scale of the regional plan, but they were no barrier to general urbanisation (which must include urban green spaces). At the scale of this sort of regional planning fairly broad decisions are being made. For example, we were not concerned how a motorway should be designed or even to suggest an alignment; but to define a corridor through which it should run, an area, however, which the engineers and I could be sure would throw up no constructional or scenic difficulties. And areas for building development were indicated without any consideration of local topography, woods or streams. The general plan was very diagrammatic, and had a rigid, arbitrary appearance. Many people misinterpreted this; and in this respect the proposals came in for a good deal of adverse criticism – 'insensitive', 'heartless', 'dictatorial'. People were seeing a plan and misreading it as a design. Maybe there was a failure of presentation; but critics had not read or had failed to understand (as often happens) what Buchanan had written. We also had to consider planning standards, particularly housing densities and open space (the two largest land uses). I remember having to argue strongly against any fixed standard for open space; the old (then 40 years or so) standard of 7 acres per 1000 inhabitants was still, to many people, sacrosanct.

Wildlife conservation was, for the first time in my experience, becoming an issue. In Langstone harbour were feeding grounds of the black-tailed godwit. In the New Forest the haunts of the red-backed shrike, a shy bird, were at risk from the growing hordes of trippers and holidaymakers. Which should have preference, birds or people? I remember greater differences of opinion among the team members over these issues than any others. In the end value judgements of this kind must be political decisions, and planners can only help to clarify the issues. But designers may find ways of reconciling, or at least reducing, conflict; and this is what we tried to do. There was good reason for concern about the forest. Uncontrolled camping, caravanning, picnicking and car parking on the open lawns and the roadside verges were producing squalour and unsightliness. Each year it was growing worse. It had been suggested that population pressure in the region was getting too great, that the growth we were planning for would have to be curtailed in order to preserve the New Forest. To me there seemed a simple solution (simple to me, perhaps, being a designer, but not so obvious to the economist and sociologist with whom I was teamed up) – to direct all these activities into carefully designed locations (away from sensitive wildlife areas and made inconspicuous by mounding and planting) and to prevent them anywhere else. So the report included some illustrative proposals for several different types of site. This idea was taken up some years later by the Forestry Commission and the local authorities with great success. Scenically the New Forest has been transformed.

Work on these regional plans was what would be called landscape planning, a term I dislike but appreciate that it is so commonly used that it cannot be avoided. I dislike it because both landscape and planning are such ambiguous words. For me landscape planning is the contribution that the landscaper (an unsatisfactory word, but I can think of none better to be the collective term for the designers, managers and scientists of the Institute) makes to land use planning. I make a strong distinction between the process of planning and the process of designing, even though both must closely interlock. Planning is the evaluation of resources, much based on statistics; it is an attempt to coordinate demands, often conflicting, on limited land and resources; its proposals are in the main written statements and its drawn plans considerably diagrammatic. This sort of plan is more comparable to a military or administrative strategy than it is to the drawn plan which is the basis of an architect's, engineer's or landscape architect's design; and it requires distinct skills and experience. But it only becomes meaningful when translated into buildings, structures, roads and new landscapes for which it provides the brief. It must be both idealistic and realistic. Designers must participate. So my contribution to those projects was such as I could bring as a landscape designer. The New Forest proposals were a very specific example. More general were the Kuwait and Kingston projects. These required the investigation and evaluation of the local possibilities and constraints (soils, vegetation, water supply, labour skills, people's needs and wishes) for the creation of new landscapes, and from these an assessment of what should be included in the master plans (the Kuwait forest planting, for example). In all the projects landscape evaluation was a large element; more so in the English examples and particularly in the Roskill Commission airport urbanisation studies, which required a quick but very general comparison between different sites.

New Towns

In 1957, together with Bill Gillespie as the senior landscape architect on Hugh Wilson's staff, I worked on the master plan for Cumbernauld; and ten years later, as one of the Llewelyn-Davies co-consultants, on the plan for Milton Keynes.

I had much more influence on the development of Cumbernauld, because I continued as consultant there for ten years or so, spending two or three days each month. Cumbernauld was much smaller. It had a more dramatic site, with steep slopes and wide views, and a harsher climate. We were trying to design the town as a totality, a small town with a strong sense of place which people could experience and feel they belonged to, exploiting both the site topography and the distant views; strongly urban in its character and density, in complete contrast with the earlier garden city style new towns. In this we were undoubtedly influenced by the general change in professional thinking (ideas tend to go in 10–15 year cycles) – there was strong current disapproval of 'prairie' new towns. One of the criticisms of Cumbernauld is that it should never have been located on a high windy ridge, in the pollution zone from industrial Glasgow. Ian McHarg said so at the time when the site was selected when he was working in the Scottish Department; and I have been told that one of the reasons he left (and then went to the USA) was that his opposition was overruled. The site is undoubtedly very windswept, with its high central ridge on the watershed between Clyde and Forth, catching the winds from both east and west; and the rain contours bend south to surround it. The regional planning studies had been carried out by the department. I have no idea what alternative sites there were. We were presented with this one, and we opted for high density and close building partly because that would be climatically better.

On the north side of Cumbernauld there was a limit to which development could spread, because of the difficulties in getting roads and sewers down the steep slope; and access from the trunk road in the valley below was ruled out on traffic grounds. So the forest, now a conspicuous element in the urban scene, came about not so much as a positive input to the master plan but as a response to the problem of what to do with land that had no other purpose. There were already some forest areas in the glen and along the south-east edge of the town, and it seemed best in that harsh climate to emulate these. So we decided to develop a forest landscape with clearings, rides and paths, something which could evolve gradually, responding to emerging demands, and take on the semi-wild and picturesque character of parts of Epping or the New Forest. The planting was carried out in the traditional way, with trees in lines and conifers as nurse to hardwoods, undoubtedly too rigid and unvaried in its early years. Conscious design for the encouragement of wildlife (just as for nature conservation in the master plan as a whole) had no part in this. But in a general and commonsensical way I think we felt that 'nature' was sufficiently provided for, in the woods preserved, in the glen with its stream and semi-wild vegetation and in this forest as it would in time develop.

Milton Keynes was quite different from the new towns that had gone before, became so much larger – a city of 250 000–300 000 inhabitants rather than a town of 70 000–100 000. Its master plan (quite as much a written statement of goals and policies as a drawn plan of land uses) was imbued with the the optimism of the 1960s, in its assumptions of increasing prosperity and rising standards of living. So it was very different in its social purposes; but also it was a very different physical plan from that of Cumbernauld or Peterborough (where also I was consultant for several years) because of its site characteristics. The starting point of the physical plan was a traffic decision, the transport consultants advising an evenly spaced grid of roads. This was possible on the gentle topography of Milton Keynes. It would have been out of the question on Cumbernauld's steep slopes; and in Peterborough too, because of the winding flood plain of the river Nene and the large eighteenth century park excluded from the central part of the designated area. So the facts of the site and its topography (crucial to any kind of landscape design) have been strong influences on all these three master plans. At Milton Keynes some architects and planners (successors to the master plan team) later bemoaned the fact that the road grid was not strictly rectilinear and rectangular. As a traffic intention it had started as a mathematically uniform diagram. As a design it diverged from that not because of any theoretical belief in or personal preference for curving lines, but very deliberately to reflect the topography, to cross the canal and river without long skew bridges and to avoid severing woods. The width of modern roads and the standard formulae for curves and gradients do, however, mean a conflict even with the gentle contours of such a site; but this planned alignment minimises cuttings and embankments.

Milton Keynes did have an ecological survey and conservation study. This was carried out, under the direction of Brian O'Connor, by staff and students of the University College London conservation course. They were more concerned with the potential recreational threat to the woods and heathland on the nearby Brickhill scarp. Apart from Linford Wood, with an unusual stand of elms and a rare butterfly, nothing of special significance was found in the designated area. But now the lakes, the roadside woodlands and the lavish boskiness of the city are producing a far greater richness of vegetation and wildlife than the countryside they replace.

I also worked, together with Michael Ellison, on the abortive plan for the GLC new town at Hook in Hampshire. Graeme Shankland and Oliver Cox (the main authors of that plan) had come up to Cumbernauld to see what they could learn from experience there. The Hook proposals had much in common with the Cumbernauld plan – the traffic segregation, the high residential density, the concentration of green space round the outside of the built-up area. But the lakes at Hook were new, made possible by the topography (there was a little stream in a gentle valley on the west side of the town) and by the need for storm water control. This need was only just becoming apparent at Cumbernauld; but at Milton Keynes, draining into a river so liable to flood, it has produced the lakes, large and small, which are such conspicuous elements in that plan.

Design Projects

Many of these have been too small, insignificant or crude in their design to have any interest for anyone but myself. Some have already been swept away by redevelopment. Some were ephemeral in purpose (like the exhibitions of 1951 and 1958). Some were abortive (including what would have been the most spectacular – the Llewelyn-Davies proposals for the central area of Tehran). Of the others most of those I have kept in touch with have been altered to a greater or less extent or inadequately maintained. The five that illustrate this chapter have been selected to show a wide range of purpose and scale. They are described later.

Many of my designs, especially in the earlier days, have included an element of what, under the influence of Robinson and Jekyll, I was brought up to think of as wild gardening; something that appealed to me. This was not quite the same as the present-day enthusiasm for ecological design – not so restricted to the use of native vegetation – but temperamentally was akin. A very early example – one of Jim Forrester's projects – was a small housing scheme on a bleak hillside in Brynmawr. In the communal spaces ash, mountain elm, sycamore, elder, blackthorn and hazel were planted; and for the grass Suttons' hay loft sweepings seed mixture was sown. That was full of dandelions, and the tenants, whose private plots were invaded by the seed, complained bitterly. I have never been there since, so do not know how the trees and shrubs have fared. A few years later there was a roadside planting scheme, Tebourba Way in Southampton. Because this consisted solely of native species, the city parks' superintendent at first refused to carry it out. Recent photographs show this to have grown well, though I am not sure that it now seems right. Thirty-five years ago the by-pass was on the edge of the city, and the planting theme responded to the rural setting; now the road is surrounded by buildings. Other schemes have not fared so well. On the whole, long meadow grass has not been liked. I know only one instance, other than my own garden, where it has materialised. Likewise there have been difficulties with plantations of whips and native shrubs, neglected and unsightly, choked with herbage; or mowing between the rows eventually eliminating the plants.

Apart from my early years in practice (when there were a few foreign students for brief spells and a New Zealander for a year or so), I have worked entirely on my own. At first this was from necessity; there was not enough design work, and much of my own time was taken up with teaching and planning consultancies. Since then it has been from choice. Working where I lived and without office costs or responsibilities for staff were obvious benefits, but I so enjoyed the designing that I wanted to do it all, down to the smallest detail, myself. And the design does not finish until the drawing is ready for printing. All that can readily be delegated (as I frequently have to freelances) are presentation and exhibition drawings. This has been made possible by the luck that I have had in the sort of work that has come my way. Large projects with direct responsibility to a client I would never have been able to undertake, but nearly all my commissions have come from public organisations with their own professional staff or from architects seeking my personal advice and collaboration. They have relieved me of direct responsibility for administering and supervising contracts, to which my input has been solely in so far as my personal expertise was needed.

Design: Sources of Inspiration

In the early days, when I was having to learn how to design by dint of doing it, I had to look around for guidance and inspiration. One obvious source was the parks and gardens of the past which, as one of my lecturing subjects, I needed to know more about in any case. Even though these places were for people and of a character that have no immediate reference to our tasks nowadays, the best have qualities, which one can absorb and analyse and try to understand, of a timelessness that is always relevant. (Though just to experience and enjoy them would have been enough.) Fountains Abbey (not just the ruins, but the long lead up to them from the eastern entrance), Rousham (the counterpart in the English idiom of Villa Gamberaia) and the Cambridge backs – all near perfect as a whole. Of other places, parts only, but these magnificent: at Castle Howard, the long avenue (switchbacking up and down the slopes – a stronger response to the lie of the land than any serpentine curve) and the mausoleum (dominating the landscape as far as the eye can see, superbly proportioned to the little hill it crowns and austerely unfussed by vegetation); at Chatsworth the east canal and view to the house (again a fine proportion, but also the interplay between the geometry of structure and the natural shape of the ground and the free grouping of vegetation); at Blenheim the grand surprise view and the spacing of house, bridge and column; at Montacute stone walls, gazebos and terraces and yew hedges linking the house firmly with its site; at Bingham's Melcombe and Levens Hall quirky individuality needing centuries to produce. Nearer to our own time little trace of Robinson at Gravetye and nothing anywhere of Jekyll. Lutyens something of a disappointment: fine in coherence of house and garden as at Sonning and Marshcourt, but generally too opulent and extravagant for my liking, sometimes too whimsical and over-patterned in detail, and sometimes, as at Hestercombe and Abbotswood, too insensitive to the lie of the land and the surrounding landscape. Late Victorian and Edwardian gardens, mostly too shapeless and overwhelmed by plants, but instructive in the mature size of trees and shrubs; but Sissinghurst and Hidcote full of lessons for garden design – their walled and hedged enclosures, the scale and sequence of spaces, the contrast of geometry in layout and structure with the free exuberance of plants, and the careful group-ings of the plants themselves: but at Hidcote poor proportions on the main axis and a disastrous anti-climax where horticulture continues beyond the gates which end the vista. Then in contrast to all this sophistication of design, the vernacular landscape of village and countryside, where at its best everything is effortlessly and unselfconsciously in harmony; and that perhaps even more instructive. Seldom are we creating landscapes that, however vast, are worlds of their own. Often we are needing to do no more than unobtrusively knit together old and new.

In France inevitably I admired the grand scale of Le Nôtre, but found Versailles too grand and in parts ill-proportioned; Vaux-le-Vicomte too precise; and I warmed only to Chantilly, with its perfectly balanced asymmetry. Italy I visited again, twice having the good fortune to stay in a late Renaissance villa high above the lake opposite Castel Gandolfo and with the distant dome of St Peter's axial on the entrance steps. I learnt to appreciate more fully how the great villa gardens belong not only to their times, but to the landscapes in which they are set – as right in their place as Montacute among its Somerset fields. This inherent fitness to people and place is characteristic of all the great landscapes of the past, the obvious lesson of history and of travel. Yet it was a lesson Kuwaitis and, later, Libyans were not wanting to learn. And was it foolish to see Cumbernauld in the image of an Italianate hill-top town? And are not the cooling and sparkling fountains so necessary in the hot and arid climates altogether out of place, save for a few heat-wave days in summer, in our rainy and chilly country?

Spain followed some years later. There I found the delicate courtyards of the Moorish palaces – elegant fountains and beautiful paving – more satisfying than the rambling gardens of the Alhambra. Perhaps this was so because I am always attracted to the 'hard' spaces; not just the grand piazzas of Rome and Venice or the elegant *places* of Nancy and their like but also the vernacular piazzas, market squares and high streets of the older towns and cities everywhere. So I dislike intensely the horticultural bric-a-brac that belittles our present-day urban buildings and, by contrast, much admire Norman Foster's Ipswich building where glass wall and paved path meet uncompromisingly. Persia, en route from Kuwait, was a disappoint-ment. The gardens of Shiraz and Isfahan (fragments only, delapi-tated, some neglected, others over full of floribunda roses) belied their fame. But there were the traditional pools, brimful with water gently seeping over their containing rims; and lines of great poplars and plane trees, dense packed along the roadside water channels.

China I know about only from Osvald Sirén's two monumental books, but like so many English people since William Temple's first account some three hundred years ago, I find an immediate appeal:

the picturesque qualities of its rambling, naturalistic landscapes in contrast with the architectural symmetry of palaces and temples; walls everywhere, from the smallest dwelling to the great fortification on the country's northern boundary; and the huge artificial hill that terminates and dominates the axis of the imperial city. I have long hankered after an opportunity to emulate that (so many of our present-day projects generate large quantities of disposable soil). Tentative attempts, though on a far punier scale, at Cumbernauld and Peterborough made little headway. Japan also I only know about from the many picture books, admiring and envying the precise perfection of the best of the gardens; but knowing well enough that moss, raked sand, absence of flowers together with garden maintenance as an art are not for this country.

In the early years after the war all the design idioms of the past were clearly of no direct relevance. We were living in a 'modern' world of 'contemporary' art, architecture and industrial design. Landscape designing had to be up with the times. Tunnard had left us tantalisingly few drawings and photographs (notably the garden for Chermayeff's house in Sussex); but there was nothing else in this country to learn from. One had to look abroad. A trip to Copenhagen in 1949 gave me ideas for a freer sort of designing, for plant grouping, for woodland and what we now all structure planting (Sorensen's crematorium at Marèberg) and for the use of a brick paving (not then to be seen in this country). A few years later a visit to Switzerland enlarged the vocabulary. Sweden was too expensive; but Frank Clark had described the new landscapes there in the *Architectural Review* and had shown pictures of what he called 'sensitively controlled naturalism' – the Swedes' conscious adaptation of the precepts of Robinson and Jekyll. America was also too far away and expensive. But one could pore over the pictures of Burle Marx's gardens – here was genuis – not for imitation (the style was too strongly personal and too completely Brazilian) but for hints on planting design. Also one could read the books of Thomas Church, Garrett Eckbo and, later, Ian McHarg, with admiration and learning much but not fully responding to. The designs seemed too contrived, in Bacon's famous phrase, 'too busy and too full of work'; and the polemic too wordy. They too belonged to their country and exemplified the cultural gap.

Professional colleagues and friends have given much help, generously sharing their experience, but it would be difficult and invidious to comment on that. Yet Brenda Colvin must be mentioned. Apart from her own garden at Filkins I never saw any examples of her work, but I doubt whether the pure aesthetics of design were her forte. She taught me one fundamental lesson – of ground form as the basis of all landscape design. I can still picture her clearly, in my first year as a teacher, at a criticism of students' work, a scheme based on an inadequate survey of a London square. She was horrified that both they and I assumed that the site was flat. In a general way it is, but she, of course, was right. There are changes of level, small but distinct; enough to produce error if overlooked, enough to lead to interesting design if appreciated. Much more important than this were the professional philosophy and values expounded in *Land and*

Landscape. She was a person of great integrity and selflessness, devoted to the cause of fine landscape that she believed in so strongly.

To sum this up (and my own experience), landscape design for me is concerned with three things. First must come the needs and wishes of the people we serve. In these days one seldom has a personal client. Even though one needs the agreement of a project manager or even a representative committee, it is not for them one is working. So who are the people, and how can one understand their needs and wishes? Complex questions, not easily answered (and more difficult in foreign countries); yet answers of some sort must be found. One is not designing for purely personal satisfaction. Then comes a delight in the world of nature – a delight rather than a scientific interest (botany I find boring – though not so ecology). But nature is to be organised for human purposes and satisfactions. So the third and controlling factor is the element of art. I have had the great good fortune of always enjoying my work, and every facet of it (perhaps because there is too great diversity for any of it to become drudgery). But the greatest enjoyment, however dissatisfying the outcome, has been the time, all too brief, at the drawing board grappling with the aesthetics of design. I would echo what Lutyens is said to have said 'God is good proportion'.

Gatwick Airport

The tiny terminal building and railway 'halt' of the pre-war aerodrome still exist, but development into the present major international airport dates from the post-war years. This is reaching a peak with the construction of the North Terminal (due for completion in 1987), not merely the buildings and aircraft stands, but also roads, car parks (surface and multi-storey), noise barrier and balancing/aerating ponds. Construction will continue thereafter, with cargo sheds, maintenance buildings, long term car parks, balancing ponds and lesser ancillary uses. And there will always be alterations to what has gone before. A major airport is a scene of continual constructional activity, and therefore of landscape change. Already there have been alterations to work carried out in the mid-1970s.

The airport is on flat, low-lying land on the outskirts of Horley and Crawley in Surrey. The plan shows how close are houses in the north and east, and two of the main concerns of the landscape design are by mounding and perimeter planting to screen the airport and reduce the sound of aircraft on the ground. Construction generates huge quantities of surplus soil, and for the North Terminal much has been used to create a noise barrier 13 metres high and over a kilometre long.

Development of the airport is much constrained by the adjacent houses, roads and railway. Space is at a premium, and the landscape design, except minimally or in very crucial areas, has to make do with the space left over from the functional layout. Much therefore is what lies alongside roads (where services and sight lines impose customary constraints), is foreground to lesser buildings such as offices, police station and hotel and is screen to the huge areas of surface car parks. Some planting of trees and shrubs had been carried out under the aegis of the airport chief engineer before 1972, but in a piecemeal and uncoordinated manner. It was in that year that the first landscape design was begun. This was for the development then being planned east of the railway, a new road approach to new arrival and departure forecourts and buildings, with surface and multi-storey car parks.

The airport was originally bisected by the river Mole, here merely a stream some 2–3 metres wide, shallow and easily wadable except after heavy rain. This has progressively been diverted to the northern perimeter where, with its associated flood plain, it forms a valley park for the use of the local inhabitants. Apart from this there are two distinctive areas. One is the surroundings and the many small roof terrace gardens of the British Airports Authority head offices, opening into an existing garden (with ponds and mature trees and shrubs) of an old house converted into a staff club. The other is woodland, planted in 1975, round the whole of the northern perimeter and part of the southern, 50 metres wide where screening existing houses and 25 metres wide elsewhere.

The accompanying plan shows the head offices (with car park to the north and gardens to the south) at the extreme east close to the access from the M23 spur. West and south-west are staff and long term car parks (the latter much more extensive than shown). Then come the Hilton hotel, three multi-storey car parks (with reserved site for a fourth) and the South Terminal with direct access from the railway. To the north of this are two office blocks and, further away, the police station. Beyond is the North Terminal with, in front of it, a hotel site, two multi-storey car parks and the terminus for the overhead track that links with the railway station. West of this terminal are the fuel farm, with its first four storage tanks, and the first phase of cargo sheds with associated office and car parks, and immediately to the north and north-west is the 13 metre high noise barrier. Further west the land is earmarked for long term car parks, cargo sheds, maintenance buildings and other ancillary uses, which are screened from the valley park by a 3-metre high mound following the line of the river, with trees planted on it. This development will have its landscape component as an integral part of the layout when specific plans are prepared. Along the northern edge is the diverted river Mole (two-thirds already completed) and the perimeter woodland. Of the land not shown on the plan there is pre-1970 development to the south-east. West of this is a narrow zone for leasehold commercial uses. Here the existing roadside hedge and trees are to be retained, but space is too cramped for the sort of woodland planted elsewhere, and the most that can be hoped for is a coordinated landscape design as each site comes up for consideration.

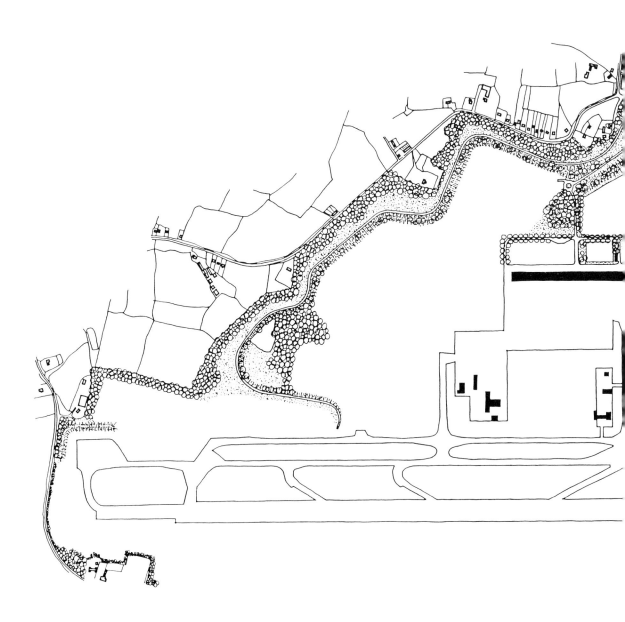

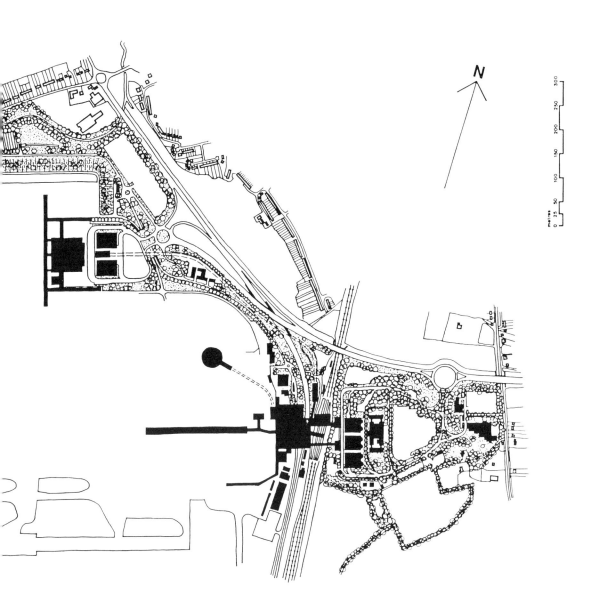

Gatwick Airport.

House and Garden
at King's Langley, Hertfordshire

The site is on the south side of a residential road which was the route to a medieval royal palace and therefore has a wide verge. This has been incorporated into the garden. It was bounded by a hedge bank (probably contemporary with the palace) which at the time of purchase was covered by a dense thicket of hawthorn, blackthorn, bramble and elm suckers. Among these were two ash and eight elms about 7 metres high. The remainder of the plot was the last remnant of a derelict meadow, bounded on the south by a public path and overlooking open, greenbelt farmland. On that boundary were an ash and a hawthorn which have been retained. To the south-east, across a neighbouring garden hedge, were visible the upper floors and roofs of a council housing estate. The ground falls evenly from north-west to south-east at a gradient of 1 in 20.

The single-storey house was designed for family occupation but with one room for my professional use. The greater part was built in 1954. Two small additions on the south side were made four years later and a larger one on the north in 1983; but these have not materially altered the garden layout. Advantage has been taken of the falling ground to step down the floor levels of the house and to construct, on the north and south side, low retaining walls. These together with the privacy wall on the west boundary and the paths and parking area are all in brick to match the house.

On the east side of the house is a hedge-enclosed area of vegetables and soft fruit, with the path, in traditional cottage-style, lined with roses, flowers and herbs. South of this are beehives and cordon fruit.

Elsewhere horticulture is confined to the raised beds north and south of the house. On the south side of the house the original meadow remains for the most part as hay field (where wild and old pheasant's eye daffodils flourish), but with a close mown area (flowery with common daisy and hawkweed) near the house and as paths to a gate beside the hawthorn and to the beehives. Scenically it would be better to have no hedge on the south boundary, so that the garden meadow could merge with the farm meadow; but the public footpath is much used, and privacy takes priority over prospect. On the north the original thicket was opened up and expanded by the planting of wild cherry, holly and hazel. The elms (fortunately, for they were growing too large) succumbed to the Dutch elm disease; and the area is now much more like a young copse (which is already beginning to yield firewood). Snowdrops have steadily multiplied and *Crocus tomasinianus* spreads prolifically and unpredictably in the sunnier places. In the shade forget-me-nots seed freely and primroses are becoming established. Cow parsley is pervasive and has to be strictly controlled. Near the house are three apple trees and a small patch of meadow bright with buttercups and speedwell in early summer.

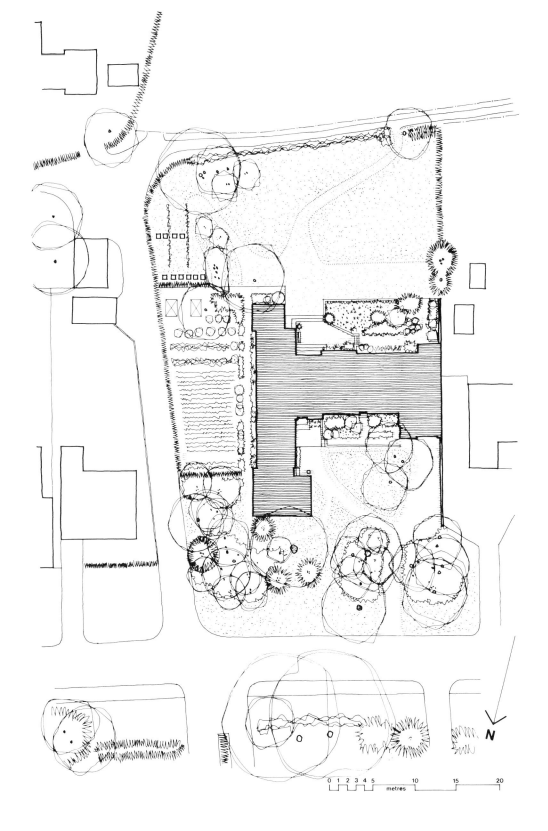

House and garden at King's Langley,
Hertfordshire.

Croydon
Churchyard Memorial Garden

Most of the site is the ancient burial ground attached to the medieval parish church of Croydon in Surrey, a few minutes' walk away from the main shopping street of the town; but this was enlarged by the demolition of houses to the north, partly to open up a view of the church and partly to accommodate a new church hall. To the east and south it is adjoined by the church school, of which some buildings date back to Tudor times. For the rest it was surrounded by two-storey houses of no great age or architectural quality. At the time the scheme was carried out it was a quiet and secluded locality; but recently a noisy major road has replaced the houses on the west side.

The ground is for the most part flat, though rising slightly in the north-east corner, and in general is a half metre above the church floor level and the surrounding pavements. Close to the church were seven yew trees and two hollies, and to the south were a copper beech, weeping ash and several elms, all around 50 years old. These were retained, though the elms have since died. Occupying half the southern area were serried ranks of tombstones and sarcophagi, of which the best were preserved and set sculpturally in low planting, with the remainder laid flat in the paved and planted sitting area close to the south side of the church. Among the tombs and trees were winding paths. These were replaced by a single gravel path leading from an old stone-arched gateway at the southernmost corner direct to the south door of the church. On the west the boundary was set back to allow for future road widening, with the railings removed and replaced by a wide holly hedge on top of a low retaining wall, the hedge reflecting the existing hollies and echoed as the backing to seats elsewhere. At the west end of the church the paved space was one of the two specific requirements of the brief (to allow for crowds on civic and anniversary occasions). The other requirement was for a lawn at the east end of the church to be used by members of the congregation for the burial of cremation ashes.

The churchyard was taken over by the borough and the scheme, intended as the town's memorial for the second world war, was implemented in two stages in 1956 and 1960. Construction work was organised by the borough engineer's department, and the planting, together with the subsequent maintenance, by the parks' department. Not all has gone according to plan. Irish yews, on alternate sides of the new path, never materialised; nor did the areas of intended meadow grass and bulbs. Some years later standard roses were added alongside the path on the south side of the church.

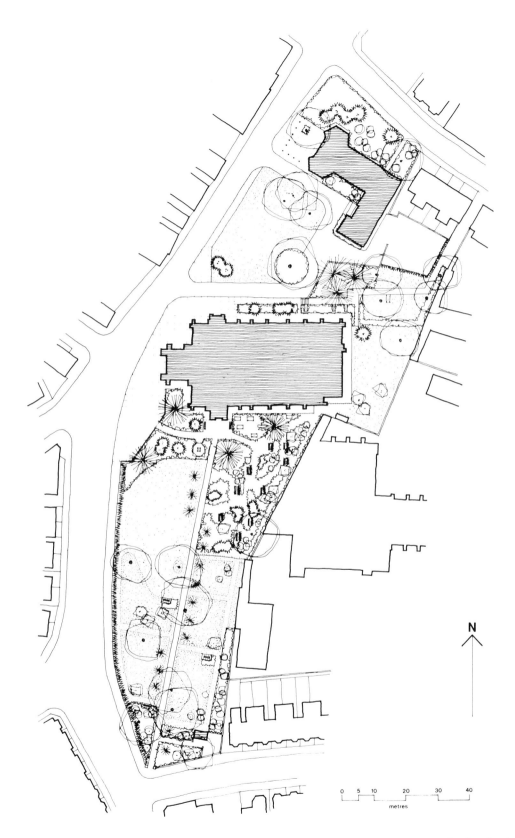

Croydon churchyard memorial garden.

Taunton Deane Cemetery and Crematorium

This is situated on the western outskirts of Taunton in Somerset. The ground falls at a fairly constant grade of 1 in 20 from south-west to north-east, with an extensive prospect to the north which allowed the chapel to be axially aligned on a church tower a mile or so distant. The site was pasture land divided into small fields by deep ditches and wide hedges that contained a few large elm trees. To the south the land was zoned for houses and to the east for commercial uses.

The design for the first stage, in 1956, was developed in close collaboration with Messrs Potter and Hare the architects for the crematorium buildings. That stage comprised the eastern half of the site. Here development had already started in accordance with an earlier plan, the access road and easternmost paths having already been constructed; and burials were taking place in the south-east. Along the south side the rectangular areas are for burials. These are relieved only by a few trees and bushes, the committee having ruled out various alternative proposals for a coordinated planting scheme as being too expensive and wasteful of revenue-earning grave space. East of the building is a lawn for ash scattering, with a small memorial chapel and a stepped paved area where remembrance flowers can be placed. North of the building is a larger lawn, bounded by an open railing along the roadside, that allows a view in for passers by and a view out into the surrounding countryside for mourners and visitors. In the original design this grass area was for the most part designated as meadow; but this was not approved. The committee also were with difficulty dissuaded from having roses planted alongside the access road, and were only placated when they realised that roses were included in the area (though very much smaller) leading to the crematorium office. A reserve area lies to the east of the access road.

The second stage, 1969, was for a south-west extension of the burial area, with a new road to serve it. Legal restrictions sterilised an area along the western boundary in front of existing houses, providing valuable opportunity for additional woodland. In the north-west is another reserve area.

The woodland consists of wych elm, Norway maple, lime and wild cherry with undergrowth of holly, elder and snowberry and fringe of goat willow, guelder rose, dogwood and mahonia. Catalpa lines the approach to the building and wild cherry the road elsewhere. Free-standing trees are horse chestnut, lime and silver maple.

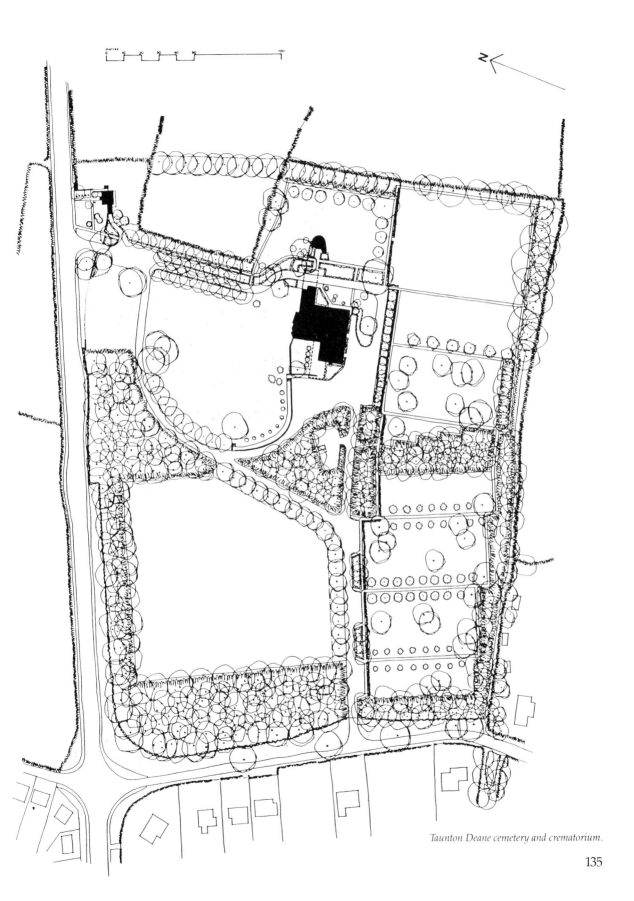

Taunton Deane cemetery and crematorium.

135

Sizewell Nuclear Power Stations

The site is on the Suffolk coast between Aldeburgh and Southwold. When purchased by the CEGB it comprised three topographical elements. On the seaward side was a low, undulating foreshore rising, in the southern half of the site, to an old cliff line some 11 metres above sea-level. This was the edge of a small sandy plateau on which were two pinewoods, on the south and south-west perimeters, and a stunted larchwood in the centre, together occupying about one-sixth of the site. This plateau dipped gradually to a small stream on the western perimeter and sharply to a reed marsh occupying the northern half of the site. Immediately west of the site was a secluded landscape of wetland meadows and deciduous tree belts, and beyond them pinewoods on the rising ground. To the north-west was upland heath which, around 1960, was planted as pure pinewood by the Forestry Commission.

From the outset it was envisaged that there might in the course of time be three stations. So the A station (design of which started in 1957 with construction completed in 1965) was set as far south as possible, but without sacrificing the southern pinewood. It was also set back behind the old cliff line and at a lower level, thus preserving the foreshore for public use and obscuring fences, roads, hard areas and minor structures, but with the pumphouse niched into the old cliff. On the south side the security fence was set out of sight behind the existing and new woodland, and substituted by a ha-ha retaining an open lawn in front of the offices. Also on the south was considerable re-contouring (using up material from building excavation and site levelling) to create new ground levels matching those of the new road. Residual areas were planted as woodland. Subsequent changes removed some of the woodland, to make way for a relocated staff car park, and added roses and rhododendrons; and the area south of the ha-ha, intended to be of semi-wild heathy character, was neatly mown.

The plan shows the A station together with a firm proposal for a B station and a tentative proposal for a C station, together with earthworks along the seaward side and additional woodland in the north. The proposals were submitted to a public inquiry that ran from January 1983 to March 1985. The earthworks emulate the effect of the old cliff line and artificially prolong it, but no longer preserve its geological form. The new pumphouses were thought to be too bulky and the old has proved too ungainly.

CEGB intentions, as expounded at the inquiry, covered also the ecological restoration of the large areas disturbed by construction on the foreshore and on the northern marshland, and included proposals for the management of the neighbouring woodlands (partly in collaboration with local landowners, partly by purchase of the Forestry Commission plantations). This management would gradually transform the woods into a more varied and uneven aged mix of species, obviating extensive clear felling and maintaining the woods as permanent elements in the landscape. For, if government authority is ever given to the continuance or increase in nuclear generation of electricity, the Sizewell site could continue in operation indefinitely, with each station decommissioned at the end of its useful life and replaced by a new one.

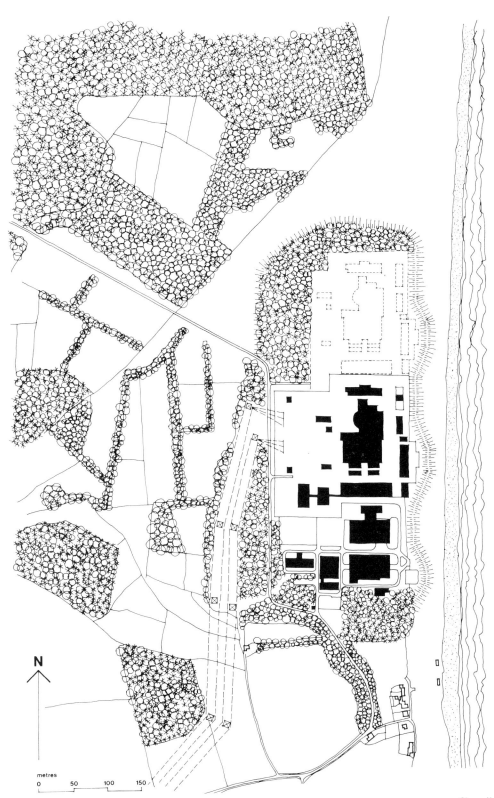

N

metres
0   50   100   150

Sizewell nuclear power stations.

Brenda Colvin *(1897–1981)*

Brenda Colvin studied at Swanley Horticultural College and spent her life working in private practice. As a founder member of the ILA, she was a pioneer of the profession of landscape architecture in this country. She was honorary secretary of the Institute from 1941 to 1948 and president from 1951 to 1953. She was awarded the CBE in 1973.

Brenda Colvin was born in Simla on 8 June 1897 and spent her childhood in India, where her father was Resident in Kashmir and later Agent to the Governor General in Rajputana. She wrote: 'My earliest schooling was in a houseboat on the river Jhelum... I remember the wealth of wild flowers and the almond blossom orchards on the lower terraces of the surrounding mountains. I remember picnics on the banks and islands of the lakes and in the gardens of the Shalimar.'

When a little older she was sent to England, where she lived with a widowed friend of her parents in one of the Grace and Favour apartments at Hampton Court; there she spent much time playing in the grounds, especially at times when they were closed to the public. She attended a variety of schools in both England and France and was fond of remarking that according to the census forms this upbringing classed her as an illiterate immigrant.

In 1920, she attended Swanley College to study gardening and market work but during the first year became interested in the design course then going on under Miss Madeline Agar, a landscape architect trained in the United States and at that time working on the rejuvenation of Wimbledon Common. When Miss Agar was replaced on the college staff by an unsatisfactory substitute, Brenda Colvin left Swanley with several other students and employed Miss Agar as tutor for a home-made landscape training course. When this was complete she worked for a short time in Miss Agar's office.

Setting up in Practice

Then, in about 1922, she founded her own practice, which remained at the centre of her endeavours throughout her long working life. For two decades the creation and improvement of private gardens were the basis of this practice, and by 1939 she had worked on about 300 gardens.

In the 1920s she was influenced by Thomas Adams, a landscape planner whose experiences in America had brought him into contact with the Olmsteds and their understanding of the wider scope of landscape design. She visited America herself in 1932, when work temporarily ran out. Thus though her practice continued to be concerned with garden design, she was beginning to think how the same principles might apply to larger projects. Her main professional contacts in England were Geoffrey Jellicoe, Sylvia Crowe, Bodfan Gruffydd and Sheila Haywood.

Her largest work before 1939 was an extensive addition to a garden at Zywiec in Poland for Archduke Charles Albert Habsburg. It is a measure of her reputation during the 1930s, that she should have received such a commission. She used to travel each summer to Poland, where she would prepare designs for the next year's work and give instructions to contractors; she constructed a new courtyard, a lake and an 'English' garden. In the late summer of 1939 she had considerable difficulty in reaching home, to a world in which creative work was necessarily suspended for a decade. Brenda Colvin had to wait a long time for opportunities which really fulfilled her vision of the role of the landscape architect. In her 20s and 30s she was working mainly on private gardens and developed a sense of frustration at the rapidity with which they tended to be modified by successive owners.

A London garden at 25 Cheyne Row, completed in 1930, where foliage plants are used against brickwork in a way which would still be considered very up-to-date 50 years later.

Planting Philosophy

Though little remains of this large body of work, Brenda Colvin was already developing originality in composition of foliage texture and colour. Many of her gardens from this period were quite conventional in layout but displayed a restrained control over plants based upon a knowledge of their form, size and texture. The ideas which were to influence her contemporaries were also developing. The grouping of strongly architectural foliage has become a commonplace in contemporary garden design; Brenda Colvin was struggling to work out compatible species for such compositions in the 1920s.

She was conscious of the need to arrange gardens both to provide satisfaction throughout the year and to reflect seasonal change. Her mastery of combinations of form and foliage colour and texture have led many to believe that her gardens made little use of flowers. This was completely incorrect; indeed, during a mild winter in the 1970s, 54 different species (excluding roses) were in flower in her own garden on Christmas Day. However, she certainly saw flowers as incidents in garden composition rather than the major framework of design. Shape and foliage were the base. Flowers, firmly controlled in position and colour, provided ever-changing highlights. Her mastery of foliage was matched by a mastery of placing flowering plants in relation to the fall of light. A small group of pale blooms would often stand vivid in sunlight against the dark hollows of shady evergreens or dark foliage shrubs.

Landscape architecture was her all-absorbing interest to which all else was secondary. This led to a life-long interest in plants, both native and horticultural, so that by the end of her life, she

Woodland at Chateau Zywiec in Poland (c. 1937) with the stems cleaned and rough grass (with bulbs in spring), a treatment characteristic of Brenda Colvin's work.

had an immense plant knowledge. She explains her philosophy of planting, so important to her work, in two articles published in *Landscape Design*, the journal of the Institute of Landscape Architects, in March 1951 and August 1961. In the latter, she says:

> Planting, for the landscape architect, includes all plants and types of plants that grow in nature or have been selected and developed by man and are available for either practical or aesthetic use in the landscape. That includes grass, trees, woodland and farm crops as well as the shrubs and other ornamental plants of park and garden. Starting from that angle we avoid the risk of thinking of plants only as decorative touches to designs conceived in other materials. The pattern of the familiar landscape in nature or in farmland and park is coloured and to some extent formed by plants, so that they must be regarded as having an importance in the design, if not in the very structure of the whole, no less important than the earth forms. So in man-made and even in urban surroundings plants are among the essential elements of the whole concept.

Between the wars another contrasting aspect of her work was also being developed. Her sense of shape in plants extended into a deep sensibility towards trees; she could see in any tree a potential beauty of shape to be achieved by careful removal of superfluous limbs. She could also see through heavy trees in the imagination and so did not need to remove a tree to reveal a hidden view; a quick marking up of lower branches to be trimmed away would result in a composition of distant space seen through foreground shade. This ability made her very interested in the treatment of the ground below trees and in the use of bulbs and rough grass as an element in the horizontal composition of gardens.

She was less interested in the design of paving and architectural elements, but developed a professional skill in handling such elements so that they were included in her gardens with a deceptive ease.

The Landscape Profession

From the beginning of her career, Brenda Colvin attached great importance to professionalism. She would sometimes compare Gertrude Jekyll's whimsical approach to her great talent unfavourably with Madeline Agar's all-round professional approach, and, of course, Miss Jekyll was guided by Lutyens and never undertook so large a task as the remodelling of Wimbledon Common. Therefore, when the Institute of Landscape Architects (now the Landscape Institute) was founded in 1929, following the 1928 meeting in the great marquee at Chelsea, Brenda Colvin was there. She records drily that the two leading landscape practitioners of the day, Thomas Mawson and Gilbert White, were doubtful whether a new professional body was needed, since their two firms could carry out all the work likely to be commissioned in the foreseeable future. Brenda Colvin could already see further ahead and helped to persuade these two masters to join the new Institute, becoming its first and second presidents. She was active from the beginning in Institute affairs, writing articles, lecturing and sitting on committees. Her tall, thin frame and distinguished profile were to be seen at meetings and conferences, shy on social occasions, but concise and unhesitatingly to the point when her profession was under consideration.

In 1951 Brenda Colvin was elected president of the Institute of Landscape Architects, and was probably the first woman to be president of any of the environmental or engineering professions. She was a founder member of the International Federation of Landscape Architects at Cambridge in 1948. In 1973, aged 75, she chaired a committee which led to landscape managers being included as professional members of the Landscape Institute; she had come to believe that design and aftercare were so interrelated that they should be represented together in a single professional body, together with practitioners in the landscape sciences. Aftercare came to be of profound importance to her thinking as so many of her landscapes had developed less well than conceived of, due to unsympathetic post-contract management. Those jobs which included a long association with the landscape's development through time gave her the most satisfaction.

She was a member of the Council of the Institute for 47 years without a break, hardly ever missed a meeting and always seemed to be in the vanguard with new ideas. In 1979, Brenda Colvin presented a paper to mark the Landscape Institute's 50th anniversary in which she noted that the profession had reached a stage where 'landscape consultants are seen as essential members of the team in almost every major work undertaken in this country.' However, she saw no room for complacency:

> There is still a large majority of the community who are totally ignorant about the profession – who have never even heard of it and seem to assume that good landscape occurs inevitably without human effort or who are not interested in having pleasing visual surroundings. Few of those who do appreciate the need for fine landscape recognise its ecological basis or its potential social role. In this matter of public understanding, the profession has not caught up with those of architecture, medicine, law or any of the longer established professions. Perhaps, however, it has an inbuilt evolutionary capacity to outdistance some of them in the long term. Personally, I believe that its inherent 'program' has a capacity for further development beyond anything hitherto foreseen... The growth of the Institute to include land management and land sciences... is a normal evolutionary development of this young art. Unless land managers and land scientists appreciate the role of design, landscape change would probably produce a different and duller or uglier setting for human enjoyment and social health. Unless designers work closely with managers and scientists who understand this, mistakes and failures are likely to wreck their work before maturity. Unless all three work together their political influence will be insignificant...

Women and Landscape

This long professional life, starting when both landscape and women were equally undervalued, and ending when both were gaining recognition, made her impatient of militant feminism. She stated her view on the subject in a letter written in 1973:

> I resist segregation of *any* sort and see no necessity for special women's organisations, as it seems to me that we exert a far greater influence in mixed bodies than is possible from opposing organisations... It is no use women crying for positions until they prove ability in sufficient numbers and sufficiently wide fields in their own spheres and develop a less biased attitude about the problem... By addressing your letter to 'dear woman Landscape Architect' you yourself make a distinction. Do I assume you would not write to 'dear man Landscape Architect'? I feel the same about your use of the word 'Chairperson'. Are you and your fellowesses all huwoman beings? As chairman of a group of human beings regardless of their sex, colour, age, nationality, religion or political views I am glad not to have to distinguish precisely as to the status of each.

Books and Writing

Brenda Colvin was a thinker and a voracious and critical reader. She had obviously been strongly influenced by the ideas and work of Sir George Stapledon FRS (1882–1960) on grassland and of Tansley on ecology, as a background to her professional work. Particular personal interests, at least in later life, were the archaeology of Britain and the philosophical ideas of Arthur Koestler; these appear to have a relationship to the philosophies of India, where her childhood was passed. She took a great interest in philosophy and religious thought; another lifelong hobby was bird watching.

This deeply philosophical outloook was expressed both in her practice and in three books. The first, *Land and Landscape*, was published in 1948. Though having a fine command of written English, Brenda Colvin found book writing stressful. *Land and Landscape* was founded upon a series of lectures delivered at the Planning School. When the second, and considerably revised, edition which came out in 1970 was being prepared, she would shut herself into her office with drafts and potential illustrations and struggle fiercely to perfect each sentence or caption. It is still a standard textbook and has been translated into Japanese. This classic work reviewed the state of the British landscape and foreshadowed today's movements towards applied ecology and countryside conservation as the backbone of a sophisticated design philosophy. Its opening lines sum up Brenda Colvin's views:

The control which modern man is able to exert over his environment is so great that we easily overlook the power of the environment over man. Perhaps we just assume that any environment, modified and conditioned by human activity, must inevitably be suited to human life. We know that this is not so, really, and that man can ruin his surroundings and make them unsuitable for future generations, just as he can make war and leave unsolved political problems leading to more war; but we continue to act as if we did not know it, and we have not properly mastered the methods which the elementary knowledge should lead us to apply.

We should think of this planet, Earth, as a single organism, in which humanity is involved. The sense of superior individuality which we enjoy is illusory. Man is a part of the whole through evolutionary processes, and is united to the rest of life through the chemistry of lungs and stomach; with air, food and water passing in constant exchange between soil and the tissues of plant and animal bodies.

Her second book, though the first to be published, in 1947, was *Trees for Town and Country* which is still in print. It describes the character and requirements of selected common trees, and has long been a standard reference.

Finally, in 1977, she published privately a collection of poems and short prose statements under the title *Wonder in a World*. This very personal work belies the dry pessimism which she sometimes expressed about the world. It reveals both her sparkling intellect and a great joy in life; for instance: 'Well may we count our blessings and be grateful for the conditions on this planet so amazingly adapted to the evolution of the creative spirit of man.'

Brenda Colvin's own garden at Filkins c. 1972. She was particularly fond of the daisies in the lawn.

Later Work

The ideas expressed in *Land and Landscape* brought her opportunities. Her practice, renewed after the war in an office shared with Dame Sylvia Crowe, received commissions of great scope. Her most creative period was between the ages of 55 and 75, during which she imagined and realised a series of influential landscapes on a large scale. An illness led her to leave London in 1965 and move her office to the house she had bought for retirement at Filkins in West Oxfordshire. However, she never retired and, from this base where the practice of Colvin and Moggridge still continues, she worked with unabated creativity.

She was active in designing industrial landscapes around the new generation of power stations and reservoirs and in promoting landscape design as fundamental to success with such projects. During 1951–2, the nature of landscape practice had changed and solutions to modern problems began to be pioneered. Between 1945 and 1968 Brenda Colvin carried out a further 250 commissions. Many were still private gardens; others included the landscape of nine schools, seven universities (one of which was the University of East Anglia), seven factories, eight power stations (including Drakelow, Eggborough and Rugeley) seven hospital or civic sites, six mineral workings and Trimpley Reservoir.

In 1962 she was appointed landscape consultant for the rebuilding of Aldershot Military Town and worked on this project for 15 years. The macadam atmosphere of the barracks is slowly

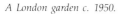
A London garden c. 1950.

146

being converted into a woodland town. This has been achieved by perceiving that on the thin Bagshot gravels, two fundamentally different types of landscape were needed. Trim grass with well-spaced trees provide military precision. In the more remote parts of the town, in a great horseshoe of higher ground around the barracks and along an old canal through the centre, woodland is being regenerated within neatly fenced enclosures. Here trees can regenerate naturally or develop from forestry-sized whips. So effectively has nature been called in to assist design, that the original budget set out in 1967 has been halved in the face of inflation without loss of content. Aldershot has also been given the basis of a new park by creating an ornamental lake as a means of extracting material to cover urban rubbish. Behind the lake there is a long hill of rubbish built in layers with gravel; the project cost less than carting the rubbish away.

Her longest term project has been Gale Common, a large hill about a square mile in size and 50 metres high, which is being built out of waste ash from coal-fired power stations in Yorkshire. The silhouette of the hill is to be terraced, being developed over a 30-year programme, towards the image which she created in 1962, grassy terraces spiralling up the steep slopes to fields and woods against the sky. These silhouettes and forms derive from the patterns created by ancient lynchets on chalk downs. The hill's derivation from landforms created so long ago and the projection of an idea as a guide for such a long period of construction unite in a single work Brenda Colvin's ideas about the connection

Trimpley Reservoir, Worcestershire. Overall view of the lower basin in its setting with the new planting and gently modelled bund of the upper basin in the foreground.

Trimpley Reservoir, Worcestershire, showing the edge treatment of the upper reservoir which is concrete lined. The rip-rap and irregular soiling were carefully designed above waterlevel to soften the margin.

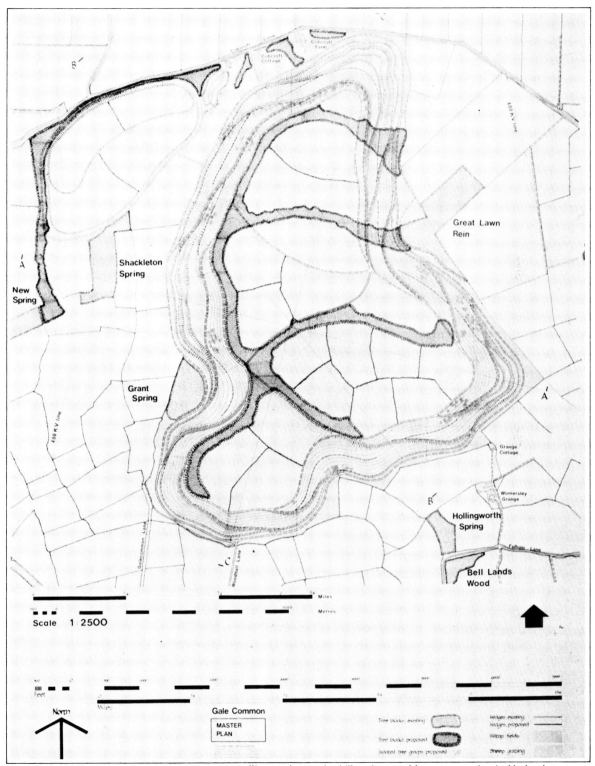

Gale Common, Yorkshire. Plan of 1967 showing spiralling tracks up the hill and terraced form at corners inspired by lynchets. The hill will be about 1 x 1¼ miles and finished in 2030.

149

between past and future, about time as a dimension in the creation of landscapes, about aftercare as an essential corollary to design.

These large and long term projects have all been created on the basis of ideas developed through garden design. She believed that each garden went to the heart of the matter of landscape architecture, posing in miniature the problems to be solved in the largest project. Her later gardens were designed with a fluency and certainty derived from long practice and thought. The seasons were under control, each entwined with texture and colour. Indigenous and horticultural areas were effortlessly combined. The form of each garden was carefully controlled sometimes with a flowing but never a random line.

Brenda Colvin kept a complete numbered list of her jobs since starting in practice in 1922 in a small red notebook. The book, which contains 42 pages, some filled double-spaced, some single-spaced, was exactly full at her death in January 1981, a circumstance consistent with her belief that life contains order beyond human determining.

> This universe of time
> This bubble in the matrix of Eternity
> Within which entities as individuals
> Are fashioned for a purpose
> To reunite at last in a new Whole:
> Unity and Disparity will be reconciled
> Within Time's spiral range, God dies for Man
> While Time endures.
> The truth repeats on many planes
> As octaves ring above and underneath our hearing:
> As light in the rainbow's spectrum widens
> Beyond the range of human sight
> So the sacrifice occurs within
> As also without our understanding.

(Brenda Colvin, 'Time's Limits')

Gale Common, Yorkshire. Corner of model showing land form.

Post-script by Hal Moggridge

Brenda's later career would not be fully described without a brief outline of her foundation of the practice of Colvin and Moggridge in 1969. As the other half of this partnership, I must write of this in a personal way.

During the 1960s her practice expanded in scope and scale. Though much helped by her senior assistant, Tim Rowell, she was feeling the stress of this responsibility becoming too heavy as she entered her 70s. Nonetheless, she wished to perpetuate her much-loved practice and so, at an age well after most people have retired, she embarked upon a new enterprise. For the first time in her life, she decided to set up a partnership. She wanted to find a younger landscape architect, sympathetic with her approach, who would be willing to move to Filkins as her partner.

The Jellicoes suggested me as a possibility and we were introduced by an invitation to dinner. I had no idea what lay behind the invitation and, though a regular visitor to the Jellicoes, was a little puzzled to find myself present on an occasion devoted to the early history of the Landscape Institute. I had nothing to contribute either as author or early member; nonetheless, the company of my evening companion, Brenda Colvin, was most enjoyable. A few days later an invitation to visit Filkins with a view to discussing a possible partnership was received. I had at the time recently started my own one-man practice.

My journey to Filkins was eventful, as at Henley I was involved in a minor car crash and so arrived late and shaken. Nevertheless, we agreed on a three months' trial period during which I would work at Filkins for two days a week, after which we would decide whether to found a partnership. It took only a few weeks for us to realise our compatibility, both professionally and personally. And so at Easter 1969, the partnership of Colvin and Moggridge was founded and from this date both partners cooperated on another 128 jobs as various in size and type as those of the previous two decades. Brenda Colvin was extraordinarily generous towards a younger partner. Large and interesting jobs were allocated to me wholeheartedly, with the advantage of the guiding hand of experience in the background.

We ran the office by working out policy over a daily lunch together, held in the kitchen or, in summer, in the garden. The succeeding decade was fruitful and rewarding for us both, Brenda being able gradually to reduce her workload in balance with her fading energy, while still enjoying complete involvement with the practice. In the early 1970s her formidable energy was unabated; my wife remembers her skipping over a fence after an uphill scamper and then helping her younger companions over the fence. She continued to work a full day, concentrating on jobs of particular interest to her. The last year or two of her life was perhaps less happy. Her mind was still as sharp as a razor, but her physical strength and eyesight began to fail, so that she lost touch with day-to-day events in the office. Though the practice gave her economic security, its presence perhaps became a reminder of earlier times when she was fully involved in it. She died at home in comparative comfort on 27 January 1981.

Bibliography

(In keeping with the retrospective nature of the text, references are to first editions where possible.)

Abercrombie, Patrick. *Greater London Plan 1944*. London, HMSO, 1945.

Adams, Thomas. *Outline of Town and City Planning*. London, Churchill, 1935.

Blomfield, Reginald. *The Formal Garden in England*. London, Macmillan, 1892.

Church, Thomas. *Gardens are for People*. New York, Reinhold, 1955.

Clark, H.F. *The English Landscape Garden*. London, Pleiades Books, 1948.

Colvin, Brenda. *Land and Landscape*. London, John Murray, 1948.

Colvin, Brenda. *Wonder in a World*. Privately printed by the Cygnet Press at Burford, Oxford, 1977

Colvin, Brenda *and* Tyrwhitt, Jacqueline. *Trees for Town and Country*. Prepared for the Association for Planning and Regional Reconstruction (London), 1947.

Coward, T.A. *Wayside and Woodland Birds*. London, Frederick Warne, 1936.

Crowe, Sylvia. *Garden Design*. London, Country Life. 1958.

Crowe, Sylvia. *The Landscape of Power*. London, Architectural Press, 1958.

Crowe, Sylvia. *Tomorrow's Landscape*. London, Architectural Press, 1956.

Dykes, W.R. *The Genus Iris*. Cambridge University Press, c.1913.

Eckbo, Garrett. *The Landscape we See*. New York, McGraw-Hill, 1969.

Fairbrother, Nan. *The Nature of Landscape Design*. New York, Alfred Knopf, 1974.

Fairbrother, Nan. *New Lives, New Landscapes*. London, Architectural Press, 1970.

Farrer, Reginald. *Alpines and Bog Plants*. London, Edward Arnold, 1908.

Farrer, Reginald. *The English Rock Garden*. 2 vols. London, T.C. & E.C. Jack, 1918.

Geddes, Patrick. *Cities in Evolution, an Introduction to the Town Planning Movement and to the Study of Civics*. London, Williams and Morgate, 1915.

Gromort, Georges. *L'Art des Jardins*. 2 vols. Paris, Vincent, Freal et Cie., 1934.

Hackett, Brian. *Landscape Conservation*. Chichester, Packard, 1980.

Hackett, Brian. *Landscape Planning*. Newcastle, Oriel Press, 1971.

Hackett, Brian. *Man, Society and Environment*. London, Percival Marshall, 1950.

Hackett, Brian. *Planting Design*. London, Spon, 1979.

Harvey, S. *and* Rettig, S. *eds. Fifty Years of Landscape Design, 1934-1984.* London, The Landscape Press, 1985.

Jekyll, Gertrude. *Garden Ornament.* London, Country Life, 1918.

Jekyll, Gertrude. *Wall and Water Gardens.* London, Country Life/ Newnes, 1901.

Jekyll, Gertrude. *Wood and Garden.* London, Longmans Green, 1899.

Jekyll, Gertrude *and* Weaver, Lawrence. *Gardens for Small Country Houses.* London, Country Life, 1912.

Jellicoe, G.A. *Garden Decoration and Ornament for Smaller Houses.* London, Country Life, 1936.

Jellicoe, Sir Geoffrey. *The Guelph Lectures on Landscape Design.* University of Guelph (Canada), 1983.

Jellicoe, G.A. *Motopia: a Study in the Evolution of Urban Landscape.* London, Studio Books, 1961.

Jellicoe, G.A. *Studies in Landscape Design.* 3 vols. Oxford University Press, 1960, 1966, 1970.

Jellicoe, G.A. *and* Jellicoe S. *The Landscape of Man.* London, Thames and Hudson, 1975.

Jellicoe, G.A. *and* Jellicoe, S. *eds. The Oxford Companion to Gardens.* Oxford University Press, 1986.

Jellicoe, Geoffrey *and* Shepherd, J.C. *Garden and Design.* London, Ernest Benn, 1927.

Johns, Rev. C.A. *Flowers of the Field.* London, SPCK, c.1855.

McHarg, Ian. *Design with Nature.* New York, Natural History Press (for the American Museum of Natural History), 1969.

Mawson, Thomas A. *The Art and Craft of Garden Making.* London, Batsford, 1900.

Mumford, Lewis. *The Culture of Cities.* New York, Secker & Warburg, 1940.

Newman, Oscar. *Defensible Space: People and Design in the Violent City.* London, Architectural Press, 1973.

Page, Russell. *The Education of a Gardener.* London, Collins, 1962.

Prieto-Moreno, F. *Los Jardines de Granada.* Madrid, 1952.

Plymouth City Council. *A Plan for Plymouth; the Report Prepared for the City Council by J. Paton Watson...and Patrick Abercrombie.* Underhill, 1943.

Robinson, W. *The English Flower Garden.* London, John Murray, 1883.

Sharp, Thomas. *English Panorama.* London, Architectural Press, 1950.

Sharp, Thomas. *Town and Countryside.* Oxford University Press, 1937.

Shepheard, Peter. *Gardens.* London, Macdonald (with the Council of Industrial Design), 1969.

Shepheard, Peter. *Modern Gardens.* London, Architectural Press, 1953.

Shepherd, J.C. *and* Jellicoe, G.A. *Gardens of the Italian Renaissance.* London, Ernest Benn, 1925.

Siren, Osvald. *China and Gardens of Europe of the 18th Century.* New York, Ronald Press, 1950.

South, Richard. *The Butterflies of the British Isles.* London, Frederick Warne, 1906.

Stapledon, Sir George. *The Way of the Land.* London, Faber, 1943.

Sudell, Richard. *Landscape Gardening.* London, Ward/Lock, 1933.

Tansley, A.G. *The British Islands and their Vegetation.* 2 vols. Cambridge University Press, 1949.

Tunnard, Christopher. *Gardens in the Modern Landscape.* London, Architectural Press, 1938.

Unwin, Raymond. *Town Planning in Practice.* London, Fisher Unwin, 1920.

Weaver, Lawrence. *Sir Edward Lutyens' Houses and Gardens.* London, Country Life, 1921.

Williams-Ellis, Clough. *Britain and the Beast.* London, J.M. Dent, 1937.

Williams-Ellis, Clough. *England and the Octopus.* Portmeirion, Penrhyndendraeth, c.1928.